Semistructured Database Design

Web Information Systems Engineering and Internet Technologies
Book Series

Series Editor: Yanchun Zhang, Victoria University, Australia

Semistructured Database Design

Tok Wang Ling
Mong Li Lee
National University of Singapore

Gillian Dobbie
The University of Auckland

Springer

eBook ISBN: 0-387-23568-X
Print ISBN: 0-387-23567-1

Visit Springer's eBookstore at: http://ebooks.kluweronline.com
and the Springer Global Website Online at: http://www.springeronline.com

Contents

Contents

This page intentionally left blank

List of Figures

List of Tables

This page intentionally left blank

Preface

About This Book

The work presented in this book came about after we recognized that ill-designed semistructured databases can lead to update anomalies, and there is a strong need for algorithms and tools to help users design storage structures for semistructured data. We have been publishing papers in the design of databases for semistructured data since 1999, and believe that after a number of attempts we have defined a data model that captures the necessary semantics for representing the semantics that are necessary in the design of good semistructured databases.

This book describes a process that initially takes a hardline approach against redundant data, and then relaxes the approach for gains in query performance. The book is suited to both researchers and practitioners in the field of semistructured database design.

Some of the material in this book has been published at international conferences. The material in Chapter 5 was originally based on work presented in [Wu et al., 2001a] and Chapter 6 was originally based on [Chen et al., 2002]. The material in Chapter 3 was published as a technical report at the National University of Singapore [Dobbie et al., 2000].

Use of the Book

The target audience of this book is practitioners who design semistructured data file organizations or semistructured databases, researchers who work in the area of semistructured data organization, and students with an interest in the design of storage organizations for semistructured data. The material is as relevant for file organizations as it is for databases since inconsistencies can also exist in data files.

Major Contribution

This major contributions of this book are:

- a comparison of data models for the purpose of designing storage organizations for semistructured data,

- the introduction of a data model, called Object Relationship Attribute Data Model for SemiStructured Data, or ORA-SS, which represents what we believe are the necessary semantics for the design of storage organizations for semistructured data,

- an algorithm for the extraction of a schema from a semistructured data instance, such as an XML document,

- a normalization algorithm for semistructured schemas,

- a set of rules for the validatation of views created on an underlying semistructured instance,

- an algorithm for the denormalization of semistructured schemas.

Acknowledgements

This work has been supported by the following grants:

National University Of Singapore Academic Research Fund
R-252-000-093-112, Building a semi-structured data repository
R-252-100-105-112, Integrating Data Warehouses on the Web

University of Auckland
Research and Study Leave Grant
Staff Research Fund, Semistructured database design

Our special thanks goes to the following students: Yabing Chen, Xiaoying Wu, Wei Ni, Yuanying Mo, Xia Yang, Wai Lup Low, Lars Neumann.

TOK WANG LING, MONG LI LEE AND GILLIAN DOBBIE

Chapter 1

INTRODUCTION

Today, many computer systems produce and consume large amounts of data. Consider a library catalogue system that stores the details of the holdings in a library and allows users to query information and perhaps even request books, or an accounting system that reads data from files, transforms it and prints reports. In the past much of the data has been stored in relational database systems and the designers of the computer systems have paid special attention to the organization or structure of this data. We have since moved to the age of the World Wide Web (or web) where many new technologies and applications have emerged. Many of the applications built today are web based, and the corresponding technologies that are used have been specifically designed for the web.

Let us consider how data was stored before the advent of the web. Data was stored in files or in databases. For the former, the entire file is read from and written to disk when data is needed. This works well for applications that do not use large amounts of data, that is, applications that can read the entire file into memory, manipulate the data and write the file back out to disk. However, this approach is inadequate for systems that require more data than can fit in main memory. For these kinds of applications, a database is required.

The use of databases leads to new problems including how to maintain the consistency of the data with respect to real world constraints. For example, suppose we have a database that stores details of students. Is it possible to ensure that a student's address appears in the database only once. If the address appears multiple times, then how can we guarantee the consistency of the repeated data? It is necessary to model the constraints in the database if we want the database system to enforce these constraints. Some constraints can be enforced by the organization or structure of the data while others must be programmed as general constraints.

Yet another problem that arises from the use of database systems is how should the constraints from the real world be captured during the design process. Typically they are recorded in a conceptual model such as an Entity-Relationship diagram. Such constraints contain semantic information, that is, they provide some meaning to the underlying data. It is important that these constraints are enforced by the database. When data is manipulated, the database system checks that none of the constraints are violated. In other words, the semantics from the real world still hold in the result of the manipulation.

Traditional relational databases which assume that data is structured are no longer suitable for the new Web applications because the data on which the Web applications are based lacks structure and may be incomplete. Thus, many of the techniques that were previously used may not be applicable. This less structured data, also known as semistructured data, is usually represented as a tree of elements, where the children are sub-elements of their parent element. Elements can in turn have attributes. Queries over the trees are represented as path expressions.

The eXtensible Markup Language (XML) [Bray et al., 2000] is a language that is used to express semistructured data. XML is self-describing since each element has a tag which gives a name for the content. However, recently, various schema languages have been defined to specify the structure of the underlying XML data and constraints that are expected to hold in instances of the XML data. The schemas are descriptive rather than prescriptive. Like traditional data, XML data may be stored in files or in a database. The database can have an underlying relational engine or it can be specifically designed for XML data. The former are called XML-enabled databases and the latter are called native XML databases. Like the entity relationship diagram for relational databases, a diagrammatic representation that reflects real world constraints could be used for requirements gathering, and for the design of schemas for semistructured documents.

Information integration is an important area that has been revisited with the introduction of XML. It is important that the meaning of the underlying documents is reflected in the resulting integrated document. Since much of the meaning can be captured in constraints, the constraints on the underlying documents should also be enforced in the resulting document. If the semantics of the underlying documents and the semantics of the resulting document can be modeled using a diagrammatic representation that reflects the constraints, then it is possible to check that information is not lost during the process of integration.

In this book, we investigate the semantics that need to be captured for semistructured data, and the different ways of representing the semantics. The rest of the book is organized as follows. Chapter 2 introduces and evaluates the various data models that have been proposed for semistructured data. Chapter 3 gives a more detailed description of one of the data models, ORA-SS (Object-Relationship-Attribute data model for SemiStructured data). Chapter 4 investigates schema extraction, examining the constraints that can be extracted from an instance of semistructured data. Algorithms for removing redundancy from a semistructured data instance are presented in Chapter 5. This is accomplished by specifying the structure of the schema in such a way that the semantics of the data is taken into account. Without knowing the constraints on the data, it is easy to define views that have no meaning with respect to the real world. Chapter 6 examines the design of views over semistructured data and the validity of the views, that is, whether the views designed are consistent with respect to the semantics in the underlying data. Chapter 7 discusses the physical storage of semistructured data, and investigates the relaxation of some of the rules presented in Chapter 5 in order to improve performance of the resulting data store. Finally, we conclude in Chapter 8 with directions for future research.

1.1 Chapter Overview

The aim of this book is to describe how semantic constraints can be modeled and used in the design of semistructured databases. The target audience is practitioners who design semistructured data file organizations or semistructured databases, and researchers who work in the area of semistructured data organization. The material is as relevant for file organizations as it is for databases since inconsistencies can also exist in data files. In this section, we give a preview the materials presented in the subsequent chapters.

Data Models for Semistructured Data

Traditional data models capture constraints such as key constraints, foreign key constraints, functional dependencies, uniqueness constraints, cardinality constraints and participation constraints, when modeling data from the real world. The constraints captured in the data models are used in the design of databases. Data models for semistructured data initially captured information that is important for information integration. More recently richer data models for semistructured data have been defined for data management.

Data models such as OEM [McHugh et al., 1997], DOM [Apparao and Byrne, 1998], and DataGuides [Goldman and Widom, 1997] have been designed for the express purpose of information integration and finding a common schema of two or more information sources. The focus of these data models is on modeling the nested structure of semistructured data, and not on modeling the constraints that hold in the data. In contrast, data models such as S3-graphs [Lee et al., 1999], CM Hypergraphs [Embley and Mok, 2001], extended Entity Relationship notation [Mani et al., 2001], XML Trees [Arenas and Libkin, 2004], and ORA-SS [Dobbie et al., 2000] have been defined specifically for data management. This chapter will review these data models and evaluate how well each of them model the constraints that are necessary for managing semistructured data.

Schema Extraction

A semistructured data instance may not have a schema that is fixed in advance. Deriving a schema for semistructured data is problematic since the structure of these data is irregular, unknown and changes often. The lack of a schema renders data storage, indexing, querying and browsing inefficient, or even impossible. Researchers have proposed some methods to extract a schema from semistructured data, and express the resulting schema using DataGuides, or a set of data path expressions. These methods extract only the structural information and ignore much of the useful semantic information.

This chapter describes an algorithm that extracts a schema from an XML data instance. Since it is not possible to extract all the necessary information from a data instance, the algorithm will indicate what schema information cannot be derived and provide questions that must be asked to derive this information. The extracted schema is expressed in a general form and can be translated to an XML schema language such as DTD [Bray et al., 2000], XML Schema [Thompson et al., 2001] and RELAXNG [ISO/IEC, 2000].

Normalization

The replication of data in a database can lead to inconsistencies in the data if one copy of the data is updated and another copy is not. In relational databases, normalization provides a well understood process for eliminating redundant data.

With the increasing amount of semistructured data available on the Web, it is important to provide guidelines for designing "good" semistructured data organizations. Several proposals for semistructured normal forms and related design techniques have been developed, including S3-NF [Lee et al., 1999], XNF [Embley and Mok, 2001], NF-SS [Wu et al., 2001b], and XNF [Arenas and Libkin, 2004].

This chapter defines a normal form based on the ORA-SS [Dobbie et al., 2000] data model. We define an algorithm that maps an ORA-SS schema diagram to a normal form ORA-SS schema diagram, and compare the proposed normal form with existing ones.

Views

It is essential to provide support for XML views so that users can view the data from different perspectives. Many university prototypes and commercial systems provide the ability to specify and query views. SilkRoute [Fernandez et al., 2000] and XPERANTO [Carey et al., 2000] provide for the definition of views over relational data. Xyleme [Cluet et al., 2001] and ActiveView [Abiteboul et al., 1999a] allow XML views over native XML files. XML views are also supported as a middleware in integration systems, such as MIX [Baru et al., 1999], YAT [Christophides et al., 2000] and Agora [Manolescu et al., 2001]. All these systems exploit the potential of XML by exporting their data into XML views. However, the majority of these systems are focus on views created using the selection operation and do not guarantee that the derived views are valid.

This chapter presents an approach to design and query semistructured views based on the semantically rich ORA-SS conceptual model. We describe a systematic approach to design XML views that ensures the validity of the resulting view. We identify four transformation operations for creating XML views, namely, select, drop, join, and swap operations, and develop rules to ensure that the views designed preserve the semantics in the underlying source data.

Physical Database Design

Removing redundancies from a data repository ensures that there are no updating anomalies. However, as in traditional databases, the repetition of information can improve the speed of data retrieval.

This chapter investigates the various types of redundancy that may arise in semistructured data repositories. One instance where the normalization rules can be relaxed is when the relationship between two entities almost never changes, and when functional dependencies hold in general but may be violated in rare cases [Ling et al., 1996]. Another instance where the normalization rules can be relaxed is when there is a recognized pairing between object classes [Date, 1975]. We investigate how the cost of duplication can be computed, and present guidelines for the design of semistructured database, which include normalization and the relaxation of the normalization rules. Finally we describe a mapping from the ORA-SS schema diagram to the nested relational model, which ensures efficient and consistent storage.

This page intentionally left blank

Chapter 2

DATA MODELS FOR SEMISTRUCTURED DATA

Traditionally, real world semantics are captured in a data model, and mapped to the database schema. The real world semantics are modeled as constraints and used to ensure consistency of the data in the resulting database. Similarly, in semistructured databases the consistency of the data can be enforced through the use of constraints. There are two approaches to designing a schema for a semistructured database. The first follows the traditional approach and captures the real world constraints in a data model. The second approach is used in the case where a semistructured document exists without a schema. Following this approach the constraints are extracted from the document and modeled using a data model.

A data model that is used in the design of schemas for semistructured data has different requirements than those used in the design of schemas for relational databases. In order to support the second approach outlined above, the data model must provide a way to model the document instance, the document schema, and identifying attributes of element sets. The fundamental concepts of semistructured data must also be part of the model. They include the hierarchical structure of element sets, and ordering of element sets and attributes. The model must also be able to represent constraints that are needed in the design of schemas such as binary and n-ary relationship sets, participation constraints of element sets in relationship sets, attributes and element sets, and attributes of relationship sets.

Table 2.1 gives a summary of the concepts that are important in a data model for semistructured data. The exact meaning of these concepts will be uncovered in later sections of this chapter and the reason we have chosen this particular set of requirements will be explained in subsequent chapters in this book.

The following is a running example that is based on the XML document in Figure 2.1. We use the term *element* to describe a particular element and a tag

8

Concepts of Semistructured Data Model
document instance
document schema
identifier of element sets
hierarchical structure of element sets
binary and n-ary relationship sets
participation constraints of element sets in relationship sets
references between element sets
attributes and element sets
attributes of relationship sets
ordering of element sets and attributes

Table 2.1.   Essential concepts of a data model for semistructured data

name in a document, and the term *element set* to describe a set of elements with the same tag name in a document. Similarly, we use the term *relationship* to describe a relationship between two elements in a document and the term *relationship set* to describe a set of relationships which relate instances of the same element sets.

Example 2.1 *In the XML document in Figure 2.1, there are element sets department, course, title, student, stuName, address, hobby and grade. Elements are instances of the element sets, so there is a course element that has an attribute code with value "CS1102", and another course element that has an attribute code with value "CS2104".*

The nesting of the element sets forms the hierarchical structure of the document, e.g. course is nested within department, student is nested within course, and so on. We say there is a relationship set between department and course, and a relationship set between course and student. Relationships are instances of relationship sets, so there is a relationship between element department that has an attribute name with value "CS" and element course that has an attribute code with value "CS1102".

Element sets have attributes, e.g. name is an attribute of department, and code is an attribute of course.

In the following sections, we will survey some of the main data models that have been proposed for semistructured documents, such as DTD and DOM, and compare them.

2.1   Document Type Definition

The Document Type Definition (DTD) language [Bray et al., 2000] and other schema definition languages, such as XML Schema [Thompson et al.,

```
<enrollment>
    <department name="CS">
        <course code="CS1102">
            <title>Data Structure</title>
            <student stuNo="stu123">
                <stuName> Zheng Zhang </stuName>
                <address>hostel 01-03-A </address>
                <grade>A</grade>
            </student>
            <student stuNo="stu125">
                <stuName> Liang Chen </stuName>
                <hobby>hockey</hobby>
                <hobby>reading</hobby>
                <grade>B</grade>
            </student>
        </course>
        <course code="CS2104">
            <student stuNo="stu123">
                <stuName> Zheng Zhang </stuName>
                <address>hostel 01-03-A</address>
            </student>
            <student stuNo="stu125">
                <stuName> Liang Chen </stuName>
                <hobby>hockey</hobby>
                <hobby>reading</hobby>
            </student>
        </course>
    </department>
</enrollment>
```

Figure 2.1. Example XML document

2001] and RELAXNG [ISO/IEC, 2000], have become a familiar way to represent the schema of an XML document. The DTD language uses regular expressions to describe the schema. In the DTD language, it is possible to represent
element sets, the hierarchical structure of element sets, and some constraints
on the element sets, attributes, and relationship sets. We investigate how these
concepts are represented in the DTD in this section.

In a DTD, the participation constraint on a child element set in a relationship
set is stated explicitly using the symbols ?, +, * which represent zero-to-one
occurrences (written as 0 : 1), one-to-many occurrences (written as 1 : n), and
zero-to-many occurrences (written as 0 : n) respectively. Element sets either
form a sequence (that is, there is an ordering specified on them) or they are
disjunctive (that is, one or other of them occurs). An attribute can be tagged
as an identifier, indicating that it is expected to have a unique value within an
instance XML document. An attribute can have a string value or be a reference

```
<!ELEMENT enrollment    (department+)>
<!ELEMENT department    (course+)>
    <!ATTLIST department  name ID #REQUIRED>
<!ELEMENT  course  (title?, student*)>
    <!ATTLIST course  code ID  #REQUIRED>
<!ELEMENT title  (#PCDATA)>
<!ELEMENT student    (stuName, address?, hobby*, grade?)>
    <!ATTLIST student  stuNo #REQUIRED>
<!ELEMENT stuName  (#PCDATA)>
<!ELEMENT address (#PCDATA)>
<!ELEMENT hobby  (#PCDATA)>
<!ELEMENT grade  (#PCDATA)>
```

Figure 2.2.   A DTD for the document in Figure 2.1

to the identifying attribute of an element set. For attributes it is possible to specify if they are required, optional, have a default value or have a fixed value.

Example 2.2 *Consider the DTD in Figure 2.2 for the document in Figure 2.1. The hierarchical structure is represented in the nesting of the element sets. For example, the second line in Figure 2.2 states that the element set course is a subelement of the element set department. The second line also specifies the participation constraint on the element set course in the relationship set between department and course, namely, that there can be one or more courses in each department (indicated by the "+").*

The third line of the DTD shows that element set department has an attribute name. The keyword "#REQUIRED" indicates that the attribute name must appear in every department, while the keyword "ID" indicates that the value of the attribute is unique within the XML document. That is, there is only one department with any particular name in this document.

The following two lines show that the element set course has subelement sets title and student. They occur as a sequence in the order specified, and every course has an optional title and zero or more students. The keyword "#PCDATA" indicates that element set title is a leaf element set, that is it has no subelement sets and instead elements belonging to this set have a value.

The last six lines describe the element set student, which has subelement sets stuName, address, hobby and grade, and attribute stuNo. Although the attribute stuNo is an identifier in the usual sense, it is not represented as an ID attribute in the DTD because the same student can take many courses, and thus, there will be many student elements with the same value for stuNo as demonstrated in the XML document in Figure 2.1.

The schema described in the DTD in Figure 2.2 represents the structure of the XML document in Figure 2.1. However, there is a problem with this

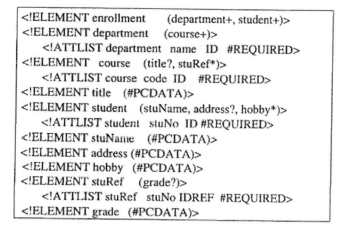

```
<!ELEMENT enrollment      (department+, student+)>
<!ELEMENT department      (course+)>
    <!ATTLIST department name ID #REQUIRED>
<!ELEMENT course  (title?, stuRef*)>
    <!ATTLIST course code ID  #REQUIRED>
<!ELEMENT title  (#PCDATA)>
<!ELEMENT student  (stuName, address?, hobby*)>
    <!ATTLIST student  stuNo ID #REQUIRED>
<!ELEMENT stuName  (#PCDATA)>
<!ELEMENT address (#PCDATA)>
<!ELEMENT hobby (#PCDATA)>
<!ELEMENT stuRef  (grade?)>
    <!ATTLIST stuRef  stuNo IDREF #REQUIRED>
<!ELEMENT grade (#PCDATA)>
```

Figure 2.3. A DTD for the document in Figure 2.1 without replication

schema. Data is replicated in the instance, for example, the details of each student are repeated for every course the student takes. This replication of information can be avoided if the structure of the XML document is changed.

Example 2.3 *Figure 2.3 shows a possible schema that does not exhibit data replication. In this schema, student is no longer nested within course. The element set student is now nested within enrollment and there is a reference from course to student. Based on real world semantics, we know that grade represents the grade of a student within a course. Thus, in Figure 2.3, grade is more correctly represented as an attribute of the relationship (or reference) between course and student.*

Let us take a closer look at the DTD in Figure 2.3. Element set department has subelement set course. Element set course has subelement sets title and stuRef. Element set stuRef has a subelement set grade and an attribute stuNo. The attribute stuNo is like a foreign key, referring to a student with a particular stuNo. Notice that there will only be one element for each student in an XML document, so attribute stuNo can be an ID attribute of element set student.

We now consider how well the DTD language supports the requirements of a data model for designing a schema for a semistructured document. The DTD describes only the schema and does not describe an instance of the document. The hierarchical structure of element sets is supported well but the only relationship sets that can be described directly are those within the hierarchical structure.

Example 2.2 illustrates one of the problems that arises through only being able to directly support the hierarchical relationship. Relationships that are not hierarchical relationships can be modeled using references. Similarly relationships of degree n where $n > 2$ can be modeled using references. However, without a direct way of supporting these kinds of relationships, valuable semantic information is lost.

Even when the DTD is small and not very complex, as shown in Figure 2.2, it is difficult to quickly gain an idea of the structure of the data without looking at the details closely.

Participation constraints on children in a relationship set are represented directly. For example in Figure 2.2, a course has zero to many students. However it is not possible to express participation constraints on parents of a relationship set. For example, we cannot indicate that a student can take many courses.

The concepts of element sets and attributes follow the same concepts in XML documents, which differs from the concepts in data modeling. In data modeling, an attribute is a property of an element set, but in XML such properties can be represented using either attributes or element sets. For example, the element set *stuName* which is represented as a subelement of *student* in Figure 2.3 would normally be considered an attribute in data modeling.

It is not possible to directly distinguish between attributes of element sets and attributes of relationship sets. For example in Figure 2.2, the element set *grade* represents the grade a student scored in a particular course and should be considered an attribute of the relationship set between element sets *course* and *student*, but it is represented in the same way that an attribute of an object set is represented, for example it is represented in the same way that element set *stuName*, which is simply an attribute of element *student*, is represented. In Figure 2.3, a new element set *stuRef* is introduced specifically for the purpose of representing the *grade* as related to the relationship between *course* and *student*. Although the new element set *stuRef* removes redundancy, it is still not possible to show that *grade* is related to the relationship between course and student.

It is possible to specify an ordering on subelement sets. In fact this ordering is possibly stricter than required since it is not easy to specify a group of subelements where ordering does not matter, which is often what we would like to represent. For example, in Example 2.2 the subelements of any instance of *student*, namely *stuName, address, hobby* and *grade* are expected to appear in that order but from a data modeling perspective we are not concerned with the ordering of these subelements.

2.2 DOM, OEM and DataGuide

Some other data models that are commonly used to depict XML documents and their structure are DOM (Document Object Model), OEM (Object Exchange Model), and DataGuide.

Document Object Model

The DOM (Document Object Model) [Apparao and Byrne, 1998] depicts the instance of an XML document as a tree. Each node represents an object that contains one of the components from an XML structure. The three most common type nodes are element nodes, attribute nodes and text nodes.

As illustrated in Figure 2.4, *text nodes* have no name but carry text (e.g. the text node with text *"Data Structure"); attribute nodes* have both a name and carry text (e.g. the attribute node with attribute name *name* and text value "CS"); and *element nodes* have a name and may have children (e.g. the element node with element name *course*). The edges between nodes represent the relationships between the nodes.

How well does the DOM support the requirements of a data model for designing a schema for a semistructured document? A DOM tree represents the instance of a document, showing the hierarchical structure of the elements, and the implicit relationships between the elements due to the hierarchical structure. It is possible to distinguish between attributes and elements. However, because the DOM represents an instance of an XML document, it does not represent schema information directly, such as the degree of relationship sets, and participation constraints on element sets in relationship sets. For the same reason it is not possible to distinguish between ordered elements and unordered elements, or whether an attribute belongs to a relationship set or an element set.

Object Exchange Model

The Object Exchange Model (OEM) [McHugh et al., 1997] also depicts the contents of an XML document. An OEM model is a labeled directed graph where the vertices are objects, and the edges are relationships. Figure 2.5(a) shows the OEM model for the XML document in Figure 2.1.

Each object has a unique object identifier (OID), a label and a value. There are two types of objects, atomic and complex. Both atomic and complex objects are depicted as 3-tuples: (OID, label, value). An atomic object contains a value from one of the disjoint basic atomic types, e.g., integers, real, string, etc. A complex object is a composition of objects where the value of a complex object is a set of object references, denoted as a set of (label, OID) pairs. We illustrate these concepts in Example 2.4.

Example 2.4 *Consider the OEM model in Figure 2.5(a). The leaf nodes of the graph are the atomic objects and the internal nodes are the complex objects. The complex object with object identifier &1 and name department is specified in the 3-tuple:*

$$(\&1, department, \{(name, \&2), (course, \&4), (course, \&5)\}),$$

where the set of tuples represent the objects that object &1 references.

14

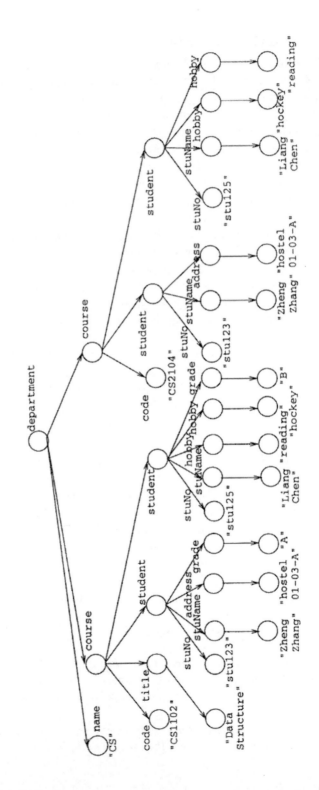

Figure 2.4. A DOM tree for the document in Figure 2.1

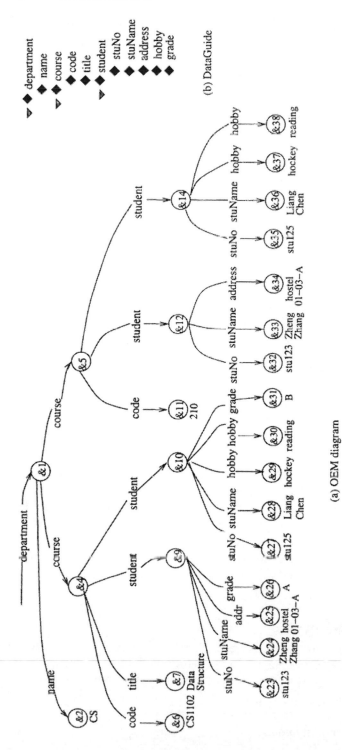

(a) OEM diagram

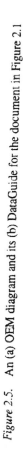

(b) DataGuide

Figure 2.5. An (a) OEM diagram and its (b) DataGuide for the document in Figure 2.1

The three atomic objects with object identifiers &27, &28 and &31 are specified in the following three 3-tuples respectively showing their OID, name and value:

   (&27, *stuNo, stu*125)
   (&28, *stuName, Liang Chen*)
   (&31, *grade, B*)

An OEM indicates the hierarchical structure of the objects. Although it has both the diagrammatic and textual representation, not only does it have the same shortcomings as the DOM but it also suffers from not distinguishing between elements and attributes.

DataGuide

A DataGuide [Goldman and Widom, 1997] models the schema of an OEM instance graph, depicting every path through the instance only once. Figure 2.5 shows the OEM model and its DataGuide for the XML document in Figure 2.1. From the DataGuide, it is easy to see that instances of the element sets *department, course* and *student* are complex objects (depicted by a triangle), where an instance of the element set *department* is composed of the atomic object *name,* and the multiple occurrence complex object *course,* where instances of the element set *course* in turn are composed of the atomic objects *code* and *title,* and the multiple occurrence complex object *student.*

How well does OEM with DataGuides support the requirements of a data model for designing a schema for a semistructured document? From this example, you can see that a DataGuide depicts only the hierarchical structure of the element sets and like the OEM it does not distinguish between element sets and attributes. It is in fact less expressive than the DTD since it is not possible to represent the participation constraints on element sets in relationship sets, and because there is no distinction between element sets and attributes it is not possible to represent the constraints on attributes that can be modeled in the DTD. It is not possible to represent references using OEM and DataGuides, which means it is not possible to model ID, IDREF and IDREFS from the DTD.

2.3   S3-graph

A Semi-Structured Schema Graph (S3-Graph) is a directed graph where each node in the graph can be classified into an *entity node* or a *reference node*. An entity node represents an entity which can be of basic atomic data type such as string, date or complex object type such as student. The former is also known as a *leaf entity node*. A reference node is a node which references to another entity node.

Each directed edge in the graph is associated with a *tag*. The tag represents the relationship between the source node and the destination node. The tag may be suffixed with a "*". The interpretations of tag and the suffix depend on the type of edge. There are three types of edges:

1 Component Edge

A node V_1 is connected to another node V_2 via a *component edge* with a tag T if V_2 is a component of V_1. This edge is denoted by a solid arrow line. If T is suffixed with a "*", the relationship is interpreted as "The entity type represented by V_1 has many T". Otherwise, the relationship is interpreted as "The entity type represented by V_1 has at most one T".

2 Referencing Edge

A node V_1 is connected to another node V_2 via a *referencing edge* if V_1 references the entity represented by node V_2. This type of edge is denoted by a dashed arrow line.

3 Root Edge

A node V_1 is pointed to by a *root edge* with a tag T if the entity type represented by V_1 is owned by the database. This edge is denoted by a solid arrow line without any source node for the edge, and there is no suffix for the tag T. In fact, V_1 is a *root node* in the S3-Graph.

Some roles R can be associated with a node V if there is a directed *(component or referencing)* edge pointing to V with tag R after removing any suffix "*".

Example 2.5 *Figure 2.6 shows the S3-Graph for the XML document in Figure 2.1. Node #1 represents an entity node, which represents the entity DEPARTMENT. This is also a root node. This node is associated with the role "department".*

Node #2 is another entity node of which database instance holds a string representing the NAME of a department. It is associated with the role "name", and it is also a leaf node associated the atomic data type "string". Hence, any "NAME" data is of string type. The directed edge between node #1 and node #2 represents "Each DEPARTMENT has at most one NAME".

Nodes #3 and #6 are entity nodes which represents the entities COURSE and STUDENT which are complex object types. A complex object type such as COURSE is connected to leaf entity nodes #4 and #5 that are associated with the roles "code" and "title" respectively.

Note that the tag on the edge from node #1 to node #3 is suffixed with a "". Hence, the relationship is interpreted as "A DEPARTMENT has many COURSE".*

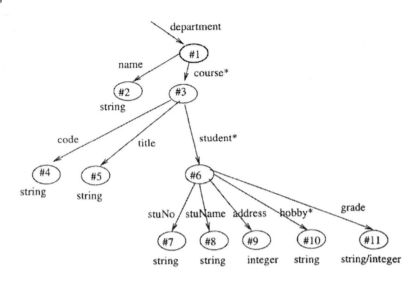

Figure 2.6. An S3-Graph for the document in Figure 2.1

How well does S3-Graph support the requirements of a data model for designing a schema for a semistructured document? We observe that S3-Graph captures the hierarchical structure of the element sets and provides for references. However, it does not distinguish between the attributes of entity types and relationship sets, e.g. it is not clear from the S3-Graph in Figure 2.6 that *grade* is an attribute of the relationship between *course* and *student*. Further, the S3-Graph is able to represent one-to-one and one-to-many binary relationship sets, and not ternary relationship sets.

2.4 CM Hypergraph and Scheme Tree

A data model that consists of two diagrams, the CM (conceptual-model) hypergraph and the scheme tree, was defined in [Embley and Mok, 2001]. The data model was designed to represent the semantics needed when devising algorithms that ensure the development of XML documents with "good" properties.

We will adopt the authors' term "object sets" when referring to "element sets" in this section. The CM hypergraph models the data conceptually, modeling object sets and relationship sets, providing a way to represent some participation constraints and the generalization relationship. The scheme tree models only the hierarchical structure of the document.

In the CM hypergraph, object sets are represented as labeled rectangles, e.g. the object set *department.* Relationship sets are represented by edges, and participation constraints are represented using arrow heads and the symbol "o" on the edges. An edge with no arrow heads represents a many-to-many relationship set, an edge with one arrow head represents a many-to-one relationship, and an edge with an arrow head at both ends represents a one-to-one relationship. The symbol "o" indicates that an object is optional.

Another way to view the arrow head notation is as representing functional dependencies. From the arrow heads, we can derive that *code* → *title* and that *stuNo* → {*name, address*}.

The scheme tree represents the same information that a DataGuide represents, namely the hierarchical structure of the object sets. The edges represent the element-subelement relationship. An algorithm that generates the scheme tree from the CM hypergraph is described in [Embley and Mok, 2001]. Because the CM hypergraph is more expressive than the scheme tree, it is not possible to regenerate the CM hypergraph from the scheme tree.

Example 2.6 *Consider the CM hypergraph and scheme tree in Figure 2.7. The CM hypergraph in Figure 2.7(a) has object sets department, name, course, code, title, student, stuNo, stuName, address, grade and hobby. The CM hypergraph succinctly models the following constraints. A department has only one name and one or more courses. The name is unique. A course belongs to only one department, has a unique code and an optional title.*

The edge between object sets department and name indicates a one-to-one relationship. The edge between department and course indicates a one-to-many relationship. The edge between student and hobby indicates a many-to-many relationship between student and hobby where hobby is optional.

There is a ternary relationship set among course, student and grade. Each course, student pair has only one grade. A student has a unique stuNo, a stuName, an optional address, and zero or more hobbies.

The scheme tree in Figure 2.7(b) represents the hierarchical structure, with department and name at the root; course with code and title are nested within department; student is nested within course; and grade is nested within student. The student information, stuNo, stuName, address, hobby, forms a separate scheme tree.

How well do CM hypergraphs and scheme trees support the requirements of a data model for designing a schema for semistructured data? This data model represents a conceptual model (in the CM hypergraph) and the hierarchical structure (in the scheme tree) of the schema. It is not possible to represent an instance of a document in this data model.

CM hypergraphs can model both binary and n-ary relationships (where $n > 2$) with the cardinality of the object sets taking part in the relationships. Notice that the hierarchical nesting is not modeled in the CM hypergraph directly. Since CM hypergraphs do not distinguish between attributes and object sets, the number of object sets in a CM hypergraph quickly becomes very large and

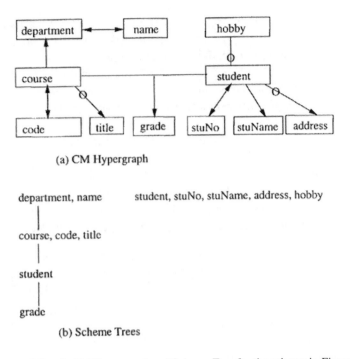

(a) CM Hypergraph

department, name   student, stuNo, stuName, address, hobby

|

course, code, title

|

student

|

grade

(b) Scheme Trees

Figure 2.7.   A CM Hypergraph and Scheme Tree for the schema in Figure 2.3

the graph very complex. One of the advantages of the ER diagram is that it is possible to have two levels of representation, one without attributes and one with all the attributes. The two levels of representation are not possible with CM hypergraphs, as there is no concept of attribute. Because CM hypergraphs are unable to represent the hierarchical relationship, it is necessary to represent it in a separate diagram, the scheme tree.

Scheme trees represent the hierarchical relationships between object sets. The hierarchical relationships can be modeled directly and n-ary relationships (where $n > 2$) are modeled using more than one scheme tree. Information about the degree of the relationship is lost.

Participation constraints cannot be represented in the scheme tree. However, the representation of participation constraints on the binary relationships is very comprehensive in the CM hypergraph but the meaning of the participation constraints is ambiguous when representing n-ary (n>2) relationships. As there is no distinction between attributes and object classes, the interpretation of "optional" is ambiguous in CM hypergraphs. For example, what is the meaning of "o" on the edge between *course* and *title*? An "o" near *course* represents that a *course* has an optional *title*. Does it make sense to have an "o" near *title,* for a *title* to have an optional *course?* It is worse if there is an "o" in a ternary relationship, such as an "o" near course, on the edge between *course* and *student*. How do we represent that a *student* is taking a *course* but does not have a *grade* yet?

It is not possible to represent any form of ordering on object sets, for example it is not possible to represent that there is an ordering on *students* within a *course*.

2.5   EER and XGrammar

A language and diagram for modeling XML schemas was defined in [Mani et al., 2001]. The language, called XGrammar, was designed with the aim of capturing the most important features of the proposed XML schema languages. The diagram called the Extended Entity Relationship diagram (EER), differs from other EER diagram notations in that it captures all the concepts that can be represented in Entity Relationship (ER) diagrams while also capturing the hierarchical relationship and ordering on element sets.

The hierarchical relationship or element-subelement relationship is represented using a dummy relationship set labeled "has". The ordering on elements is expressed as a solid line between the relationship set and the ordered entity set. The authors use the term "entity sets" when referring to "element sets". Entity sets are represented as rectangles and relationship sets by diamonds on the edges.

Example 2.7 *Consider the EER diagram in Figure 2.8(a) with entity sets Department, Course and Student. Department has a key attribute called name. Course has a key attribute code, and a single valued attribute title. Student has a key attribute stuNo, single valued attributes stuName and address, and a multi-valued attribute hobby. There are two relationship sets with the label "has", representing a hierarchical relationship between entity sets Department and Course, and another between entity sets Course and Student. The latter has an attribute grade. A department has one or more courses, and a course belongs to only one department. A course has zero or more students and a student belongs to one or more courses.*

Ordering of entities is represented by a bold line in an EER diagram. The requirement that students taking a course must occur in a particular order is represented in Figure 2.9.

The language XGrammar is able to express the hierarchical relationship between entity sets, distinguish attributes from elements, represent participation constraints on the children elements, and represent references. An XGrammar definition of the schema in Example 2.7 is described in Example 2.8. The XGrammar language describes the entity sets and the constraints imposed on them as a 5-tuple {N,T,S,E,A}, where:

1 N is a set of non-terminal symbols, which represent the entity sets.

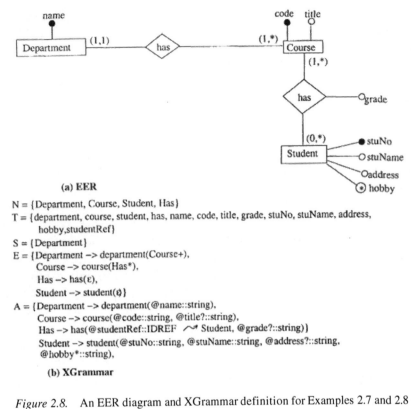

(a) EER

N = {Department, Course, Student, Has}
T = {department, course, student, has, name, code, title, grade, stuNo, stuName, address,
    hobby,studentRef}
S = {Department}
E = {Department –> department(Course+),
    Course –> course(Has*),
    Has –> has(ε),
    Student –> student(∅)}
A = {Department –> department(@name::string),
    Course –> course(@code::string, @title?::string),
    Has –> has(@studentRef::IDREF ⤳ Student, @grade?::string)}
    Student –> student(@stuNo::string, @stuName::string, @address?::string,
    @hobby*::string),

(b) XGrammar

Figure 2.8. An EER diagram and XGrammar definition for Examples 2.7 and 2.8

2 T is a set of terminal symbols, which represent instances of the entity sets and attributes.

3 S is the non terminal symbol representing the document root.

4 E is a set of production rules describing the relationship between the entity sets.

5 A is a set of production rules describing attributes.

The production rules in E and A express the constraints of interest. The authors use the notation ϵ, ~>, and @ to express an empty subelement, a reference, and an attribute respectively.

Example 2.8 *Consider the XGrammar definition in Figure 2.8(b). The set N contains the names of the entity sets, Department, Course and Student, as well as an entity set Has. The relationship set "has" between entity sets Course and Student is modeled as an entity set in the XGrammar definition because it has an attribute, grade.*

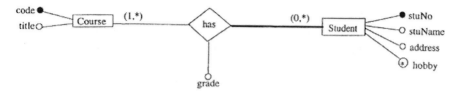

Figure 2.9. An EER diagram and XGrammar definition representing ordering on student within course

Just as in relational data modeling where many-to-many relationships with an attribute are captured in a separate relation, XGrammar models many-to-many relationships with an attribute as a separate entity set. The other "has" relationship set between Department and Course is a one-to-many relationship and is captured in the nesting of Course within Department. The set T contains the entities and attributes. S contains the entity set that is the root of the tree.

The set E specifies the relationship sets on the entity sets. The first rule in E specifies that entity set Department has one or more Courses. Recall the Department represents the entity set while department represents an entity or instance of Department. The second rule specifies that and entity belonging to the entity set Course has zero or more entities of the entity set Has as subelements. The third and fourth rules specify that the entity sets Has and Student have no children. This is represented by the ε.

As mentioned above, we have included the entity set Has in the XGrammar definition to deal with the relationship attribute grade. The constraints on attributes are described in set A. An @ denotes an attribute. Entity set Department has an attribute name which is of type string. Entity set Course has two attributes code, and title which is optional. Entity set Has has attributes studentRef which is a reference to Student denoted by ~>, and grade which is optional. Entity set Student has attributes stuNo, stuName, address which is optional, and hobby which is a multi-valued attribute.

How well does the EER and XGrammar support the requirements of a data model for designing a schema for semistructured data? The EER diagram and XGrammar serve different purposes and can in turn represent different concepts. It is not possible to represent an instance of an XML document using EER or XGrammar. In an EER diagram it is not possible to represent which entity set is the root of the tree. There is a problem with representing the hierarchical structure of a semistructured schema in the EER diagram. The relationship set "has" is used to express the hierarchical structure, but this relationship set has no direction so it is unclear which entity set is the element and which is the subelement in the relationship set. So the relationship set "has" cannot represent the hierarchical structure directly. As shown in Figure 2.8(a) there can be more than one "has" relationship types in an EER diagram.

The hierarchical structure can be represented in XGrammar, but like the DTD, XGrammar represents the hierarchical structure as a binary relationship only. It is possible to represent n-ary as well as binary relationships in the EER diagram but because n-ary relationships were not considered in [Mani et al., 2001], the authors have not considered any implications of these relationships in the algorithms that they specify. It is possible to represent the participation constraints of both child and parent entity sets in the EER diagram, but not in XGrammar. It is possible to show that an attribute is a key or identifying attribute in the EER diagram but it is not possible to show whether other attributes are mandatory or optional. One way to overcome this problem is to represent attributes as entity sets but this could lead to many more entity sets than are really needed. It is not possible to represent identifying attributes in XGrammar.

Like in ER diagrams, it is possible to represent attributes of relationship sets in the EER diagram and there is also an extension to represent ordering on elements. However, there is no distinction between attributes of entity sets and attributes of relationship sets in XGrammar. Also, it is not possible to represent ordering directly in XGrammar. It is not possible to represent ordering on attributes in EER diagrams or XGrammar, except to represent ordered attributes as elements. A distinction is made between attributes and elements in both EER diagrams and XGrammar. The concept of attribute here is the same as that in ER diagrams which differs from the concept in XML documents, so some of the attributes in the EER diagram might be modeled as elements in an XML document.

From the examples and discussion, we can see that EER diagrams are better for conceptual modeling while the XGrammar language is more appropriate for specifying the "implementation" details of the schema. For example in Figure 2.8, information such as there is a many-to-many relationship set between entity sets *Course* and *Student* is lost in the XGrammar model. The fact that *grade* is an attribute of the relationship set between entity sets *Course* and *Student* is also lost. These concepts are modeled using an entity set *Has* and a reference, but the reason for modeling these concepts in this way are not recorded in the XGrammar model.

2.6   AL-DTD and XML Tree

Arenas and Libkin describe a data model that they later use to define a normal form called XNF [Arenas and Libkin, 2004]. In the data model, they define languages for describing an XML Tree and a DTD. In this section we will refer to the DTD defined by Arenas and Libkin as the AL-DTD to avoid confusion.

V = {v0, v1, v2, v3, v4, v5, v6, v7, v8, v9, v10, v11, v12, v13, v14, v15, v16, v17,v18,v19}

lab(v0) = department	ele(v0) = [v1, v12]	att(v0, @name) = "CS"
lab(v1) = course	ele(v1) = [v2, v3, v7]	att(v1, @code) = "CS1102"
lab(v2) = title	ele(v2) = "Data Structure"	att(v3, @stuNo) = "stu123"
lab(v3) = student	ele(v3) = [v4, v5, v6]	att(v7, @stuNo) = "stu125"
lab(v4) = stuName	ele(v4) = "Zheng Zhang"	att(v12, @code) = "CS2104"
lab(v5) = address	ele(v5) = "hostel 01–03–A"	att(v13, @stuNo) = "stu123"
lab(v6) = grade	ele(v6) = "A"	att(v16, @stuNo) = "stu125"
lab(v7) = student	ele(v7) = [v8, v9, v10, v11]	
lab(v8) = stuName	ele(v8) = "Liang Chen"	
lab(v9) = hobby	ele(v9) = "hockey"	
lab(v10) = hobby	ele(v10) = "reading"	
lab(v11) = grade	ele(v11) = "B"	
lab(v12) = course	ele(v12) = [v13, v16]	
lab(v13) = student	ele(v13) = [v14, v15]	
lab(v14) = stuName	ele(v14) = "Zheng Zhang"	
lab(v15) = address	ele(v15) = "hostel 01–03–A"	
lab(v16) = student	ele(v16) = [v17, v18, v19]	
lab(v17) = stuName	ele(v17) = "Liang Chen"	
lab(v18) = hobby	ele(v18) = "hockey"	
lab(v19) = hobby	ele(v19) = "reading"	

Figure 2.10. A textual representation of the XML Tree in Figure 2.11

An XML Tree is defined precisely in a textual description which can be shown diagrammatically as a tree. The internal nodes are labeled with identifiers, and the leaf nodes are labeled with the value of an attribute or element set.

The textual description is represented as T = (V, lab, ele, att, root) where:

1 V is the set of node identifiers,

2 lab is a mapping from the node identifiers to the names of the element sets and attributes,

3 ele is a mapping from the node identifiers to a list of node identitiers or a string,

4 att is a mapping from the node identifier and attribute name to the value of the attribute.

Example 2.9 *Consider the XML Tree in text format in Figure 2.10 and the diagrammatic representation in Figure 2.11.*

In the diagrammatic representation, identifiers are assigned to the internal nodes of the tree. These identifiers are in turn used in the textual representation

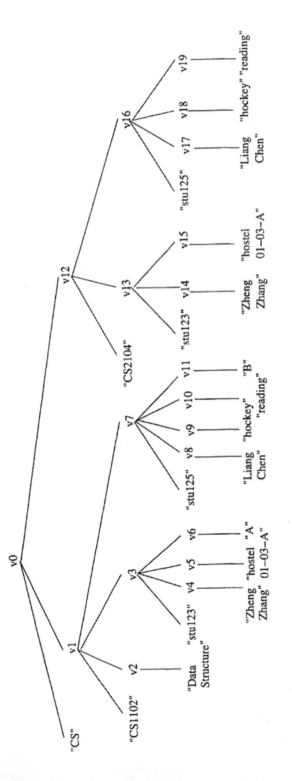

Figure 2.11. A diagram of the XML Tree in Figure 2.10

of the document instance. V is the set of vertices, or node identifiers. The labels in the mapping lab correspond to the values of the tags in the original XML document. These labels include department, course, title, etc. lab provides the mapping from node identifiers to labels.

The mapping ele maps from a node identifier to either a string value (e.g. ele(v2) = "Data Structures") indicating that the node (v2) is a leaf node or a list of node identifiers (e.g. ele(v0) = [v1, v12]) indicating that the node (vo) is a non-leaf node with children (v1 and v12 in this case).

The mapping att maps the node id and attribute name to the value of the attribute. For example, the mapping att(v0, @name) = "CS" shows that node with id v0 has an attribute called name with value "CS".

One of the deficiencies of the textual representation is that it is difficult to visualize the data and their relationships. The node identifiers in the diagrammatic representation and in *V* in the textual representation are introduced and bear no relationship to the original XML document. The diagrammatic representation alone also has a number of deficiencies. In particular, the labels of nodes and attribute names are not shown; the relationships captured are binary relationships; and it is not possible to distinguish between attributes of elements and attributes of relationships, e.g. *stuName* and *grade* are represented in the same way. Notice that the ordering of the children is significant.

The schema of the XML Tree, represented in an AL-DTD, can be represented precisely in a language that captures similar semantics to the document type definition (DTD) language [Bray et al., 2000].

The AL-DTD is represented as D = (E, A, P, R, r) where:

1 E is a set of element sets,

2 A is a set of attributes,

3 P is a mapping from element sets to the children of the element sets, indicating the participation constraints on children,

4 R is a mapping from element sets to attributes, indicating which element set the attribute belongs to,

5 r is the name of the root element set.

Example 2.10 *Consider the AL-DTD in Figure 2.12. The set E contains all the element sets, such as department, course, title, etc. and the set A contains all the attributes, such as name, code, stuNo. The set r contains the root element set, department. P maps from the element sets to the children of the element sets, for example course has children title and studentRef(s). Department must have at least one course, represented as course, course*.*

28

E ={department, course, title, student, stuName, address, hobby, grade, studentRef}
A = { @name, @code, @stuNo}   P(address) = S
r = department   P(hobby) = S
P(department) = course, course*,student*   P(grade) = S
P(course) = title, studentRef*   R(department) = { @name}
P(title) = S   R(course) = { @code}
P(student) = stuName, address, hobby*   R(student) = { @stuNo}
P(studentRef) = grade   R(studentRef) = { @stuNo}
P(name) = S

Figure 2.12. An AL-DTD schema for the XML Tree in Figures 2.10 and 2.11

An element set that has a string value is mapped to S, which corresponds to PCDATA in the DTD. R which is the mapping from element sets to attributes shows that element set department has attribute name etc.

How well does the AL-DTD and XML Tree support the requirements of a data model for designing a schema for semistructured data? This data model is able to succinctly and precisely represent both the instance and schemas of XML documents. However, since it is based on XML documents, it has the same shortcomings as XML. While it handles hierarchical relationships nicely, it is not possible to represent many-to-many and many-to-one relationships. It is not possible to distinguish between binary and n-ary ($n > 2$) relationships and there is also no distinction between attributes of element sets and attributes of relationships. The AL-DTD does not show identifying attributes, and because the schema is modeled as a tree it is not possible to model IDREF or IDREFS from the DTD language directly. The AL-DTD is less expressive than the DTD language.

2.7   ORA-SS

The ORA-SS data model [Dobbie et al., 2000] has four basic concepts: object classes, relationship types, attributes and references, and consists of four diagrams: the schema diagram, the instance diagram, the functional dependency diagram and the inheritance diagram. Notice that "element sets" are called "object classes" in the ORA-SS data model, and "relationship sets" are called "relationship types".

The ORA-SS instance diagram is like a DOM tree, in that it captures the instance of a document. However, it is unlike the DOM tree in that it is possible to distinguish between attributes and object classes. The ORA-SS schema diagram, which captures the schema information, is like the CM hypergraph, except that it is semantically richer. The functional dependency diagram captures functional dependencies that cannot be expressed in the participation constraints in the schema diagram, such as those of n-ary relationships, and the inheritance diagram captures ISA relationships.

Consider the ORA-SS instance diagram in Figure 2.13. An ORA-SS instance diagram has two kinds of nodes, internal and leaf nodes. Internal or non-leaf nodes are represented as labeled rectangles, and leaf nodes are labeled circles that have a value. The rectangles represent objects and the circles represent attributes and their values. Attributes in the ORA-SS sense are like attributes in an ER diagram which is not the same as attributes in XML documents. Attributes in ORA-SS may be represented as elements or attributes in an XML document. ORA-SS instance diagrams can be used when an XML document exists but the schema of the document is unknown. Some schema information can be extracted from the instance diagram while other semantic information and constraints must be sought from a domain expert. See Chapter 4 for details.

Consider the ORA-SS schema diagram in Figure 2.14. An object class is represented as a labeled rectangle. A relationship type between object classes in an ORA-SS schema diagram can be described by *name (object class list), n, p, c,* where *name* denotes the name of the relationship type, *object class list* is the list of objects participating in the relationship type, *n* is an integer indicating the degree of the relationship type (n=2 indicates binary, n=3 indicates ternary, etc.), *p* is the participation constraint (the cardinality of the mapping between object classes) of the parent object class in the relationship type, and *c* is the participation constraint of the child object class. The *name* is optional. The *object class list* is included only if the object classes participating in the relationship type are separated by some other object class(es) not relevant to the relationship type in the path which includes all participating object classes of the relationship type. The participation constraints are defined using the *min:max* notation, also used in the EER diagram. The symbols ?, *, + are shorthand notations and have the same meaning as they have in DTDs. An edge between two object classes can have more than one such relationship type label to indicate the different relationship types the object classes participate in.

Attributes of object class or relationship type are denoted by labeled circles. Some object classes may have identifiers, which are denoted as filled circles. An attribute can be mandatory or optional, single-valued or multivalued. All attributes are assumed to be mandatory and single-valued, unless the circle contain an ?, which shows that the are single valued and optional, or a + which shows that they are multivalued and required, or an * which shows they are optional multivalued attributes. Attributes of an object class can be distinguished from attributes of a relationship type. The former has no label on its incoming edge while the latter has the name of the relationship type to which it belongs on its incoming edge.

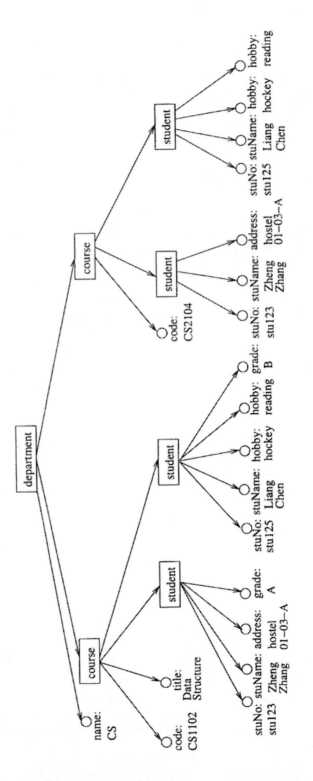

Figure 2.13. An ORA-SS Instance Diagram for the document in Figure 2.1

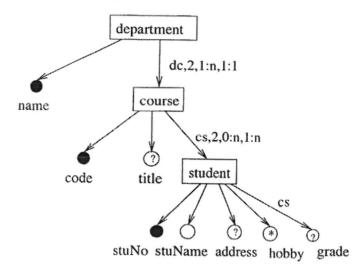

Figure 2.14. An ORA-SS schema diagram for the document in Figure 2.1

Example 2.11 *Consider the ORA-SS instance diagram in Figure 2.13. The labeled rectangles represent objects, for example, there are objects department, course and student. The labeled circles represent attributes, for example there is an attribute code with value "CS1102", and the attribute title with value "Data Structure".*

Figure 2.14 show the ORA-SS schema diagram. The rectangles labeled department, course and student are examples of object classes. Attributes name, code and stuNo are the identifiers of the object class department, course and student respectively. The meaning of identifier in the ORA-SS is the same as the identifier of an entity type in the ER sense, that is, the attribute has a unique value in the real world. For example, every student has a unique stuNo. Each of the attributes title, address, hobby and grade are optional. Attribute hobby is multivalued, and attribute stuName is required.

There are two relationship types, called dc and cs. Relationship type dc represents a binary relationship between object classes department and course, and cs represents another binary relationship between course and student. A department can have one or more courses, and a course belongs to one and only one department. A course can have zero or more students, and a student can take 1 or more courses. The label cs on the edge between student and grade indicates that grade is a single valued attribute of the relationship type cs. That is, the attribute grade is the attribute of a student in a course. From these constraints, we can derive that

$$course, \ student \rightarrow grade.$$

Some of the information in the label is redundant so it is not necessary to include all the fields. For example the label for relationship type dc can be shortened to *2,+,1:1,* since we do not need to use the name of the relationship type elsewhere and it is obvious that the relationship type is between object classes *department* and *course.*

How well does the ORA-SS data model support the requirements of a data model for designing a schema for semistructured data? The hierarchical structure of the object classes is clearly shown in the ORA-SS schema diagram, along with participation constraints on parent and children object classes. A distinction is made between attributes of object classes and attributes of relationship types. An attribute that belongs to a relationship type has the name of the relationship type on its incoming edge where an attribute that belongs to an object class has no label on its incoming edge. Compare for example the attributes *address* and *grade.* Attribute *address* is an attribute of *student* where attribute grade is an attribute of the relationship type *cs* where the participating object classes are *course* and *student.* In Figure 2.14 we depict only binary relationships but it is also possible to represent n-ary relationship types ($n > 2$) in ORA-SS schema diagrams.

Example 2.12 *The ORA-SS schema diagram in Figure 2.15 shows a relationship type between student and course called sc. Attribute grade is an attribute of relationship type sc. The attribute grade models the grade that a student gains in a course. There is a binary relationship type between course and tutor called ct, with an attribute hours. The attribute hours models the hours a tutor spends on a course per week. Finally there is a relationship type called sct among object classes student, course and tutor. It is a ternary relationship. Attribute feedback, which belongs to relationship type sct, models the feedback a tutor gets on a course from a student.*

It is also possible to depict orderings on attributes or elements. For example if students are to be ordered within a course, this is depicted by a < in the label, and if hobbies are ordered by priority this is depicted by a < on the incoming edge as shown in Figure 2.16.

A more detailed description of the ORA-SS data model in given in Chapter 3.

2.8 Discussion

In this chapter, we have listed the features that are required in XML data models to support the design of schemas for XML documents. We have de-

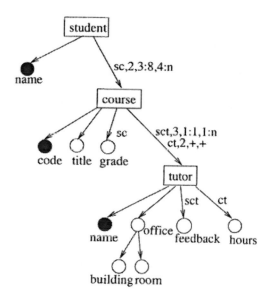

Figure 2.15. An ORA-SS schema diagram showing binary and ternary relationships

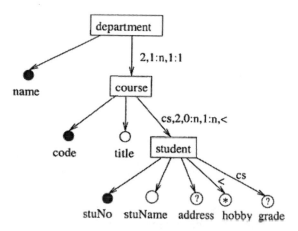

Figure 2.16. An ORA-SS schema diagram showing ordering of students and hobbies

scribed the major data models that have been proposed for modeling schemas for semistructured documents. Table 2.2 summarizes the findings of this chapter. In this table, a $\sqrt{}$ indicates the data model supports the feature, a $\times$ indicates that data model does not support the feature, while a $\sqrt{}/\times$ indicates that the feature is partially supported or the feature is not directly supported but it is possible to model it.

	DTD	DOM	OEM	S3-graph	CM	EER	XMLTree	ORA-SS
instance	×	√	√	×	×	×	√	√
schema	√	×	√	√	√	√	√	√
identifying attribute	√×	×	×	×	×	√×	×	√
hierarchical relationship	√	√	√	√	√	√×	√	√
nary relationship	×	×	×	×	√	√	×	√
participation constraints	√×	×	×	√×	√×	√	√×	√
references	√×	×	×	√×	×	√	√×	√
attributes and elements	√×	√	×	√	×	√	√	√
relationship attributes	×	×	×	×	√×	√	×	√
ordering	√×	×	×	×	×	√	√×	√

Table 2.2. Features supported in XML Data Models

A DTD does not model the instance of the data, and the only relationships that can be modeled using the DTD are binary relationships in the hierarchical structure or references. It is possible to indicate the participation of the children in hierarchical relationships and the participation of the referenced elements. No distinction is made between attributes of elements and attributes of elements, and there is always an ordering on subelements since they are represented as a sequence.

A DOM represents an instance of an XML document, so it is not possible to represent information about the schema other than the hierarchical structure. A DOM does distinguish between attributes and elements. The OEM again represents an instance of an XML document, but unlike the DOM it does not distinguish between attributes and elements. With DataGuides, the hierarchy of object sets is represented explicitly. An inadequacy of the DataGuide is its inability to express the degree of n-ary relationships for the hierarchical semistructured data, which introduces ambiguous data representations.

The S3-graph does not model the instance of an XML document, but captures the hierarchical structure of semistructured data. It does not provide for the specification of the identifying attribute of an entity, and does not distinguish between attributes of objects and relationships. The S3-graph is not able to depict the degree of relationships, and cannot capture relationships beyond the binary one-to-one and one-to-many relationships.

The CM hypergraph and scheme tree data model has no way to represent a data instance, does not provide a way to model references, does not distinguish between objects and attributes, has no way of representing ordering, and the conceptual information and nesting relationships are in two separate diagrams. Participation constraints and the distinction between attributes of relationships and attributes of elements can be modeled in CM hypergraphs.

Using the EER and the XGrammar data model it is not possible to represent a data instance, and the representation of hierarchy in the EER diagram is ambiguous without other information. While it is possible to represent many of the other features, it is sometimes necessary to have both the EER representation and the XGrammar representation to gain a clear understanding of the exact semantics. For example, if a relationship is modeled using references in the XGrammar representation then some participation constraint information is lost. Also, XGrammar does not distinguish between attributes of object classes and attributes of relationship types, and XGrammar is unable to represent the degree of relationship types. Because it is not possible to model all the constraints in either EER or XGrammar, both representations are required to model the semantics needed to effectively manage semistructured data.

The data model presented in [Arenas and Libkin, 2004] describes a language for specifying an instance, (i.e. the XML Tree), a diagram for representing the instance and a language for specifying the schema (i.e. the AL-DTD). The specification of the instance, represents the hierarchical structure of the XML instance, the values of elements and attributes, and the ordering on elements. The language for specifying the schema captures most of the of the DTD language, except ID and IDREF(S). Consequently it is not possible to specify an n-ary relationship where $n > 2$, it is not possible to specify the participation constraint of a parent element in a relationship, and it is not possible to distinguish between attributes of element sets and attributes of relationship types.

In summary, the major advantages of ORA-SS over existing semistructured data models for designing schemas for semistructured data are its ability to represent the data instance, distinguish between attributes and object classes, differentiate between attributes of object classes and attributes of relationship types, and to express the degree of relationship types and the participation constraints on the object classes in the relationship types. Such expressed information is important, even crucial for designing "good" semistructured databases, and defining meaningful semistructured views.

This page intentionally left blank

Chapter 3

ORA-SS

The ORA-SS data model has three basic concepts: object classes, relationship types and attributes. Object classes model sets of real world entities. An object class is related to other object classes through relationship types. Attributes are properties, and may belong to an object class or a relationship type. The ORA-SS data model consists of four diagrams: ORA-SS instance diagram, ORA-SS schema diagram, functional dependency diagram and ORA-SS inheritance diagram. The instance diagram provides a way to visualize an instance of the data, the schema diagram represents the structure and constraints on an instance, additional functional dependencies can be represented in the functional dependency diagram and specialization/generalization relationships among the object classes are represented in the inheritance diagram.

3.1   ORA-SS Schema Diagram

An ORA-SS schema diagram is a directed graph where each internal node is an object class, and each leaf node is a complex attribute or an attribute. The focus of this section is to describe what can be expressed using the ORA-SS schema diagram. The various notations are summarized in Appendix A.

Object Class

An object class represents a set of entities in the real world, and is similar to an entity type in an ER diagram, a class in an object-oriented diagram or the type of an element in the semistructured data model. An object class is represented by a labeled rectangle. The label shows the name of the object class (inside the rectangle). The name is mandatory. The attributes are represented as labeled circles joined to their object class by a directed edge and identifiers are filled circles. An identifier is a concept borrowed from the object oriented

38

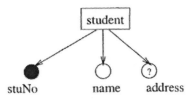

Figure 3.1. Object class *student* with attributes in an ORA-SS Schema Diagram

model, where an identifier value can identify an object. Both attributes and identifiers are described in more detail later in this chapter.

An entity type in an ER diagram typically has a name and is characterized by the set of attributes that belong to each entity. Since semistructured data is less regular than traditional (structured) data, the object classes are characterized by a name rather than a set of attributes. The set of attributes associated with an object class are the attributes that instances of that object class could have. However, there is no expectation that every instance of an object class should have a value for each attribute.

Example 3.1 *Consider modeling a set of students where each student has a stuNo, a name and might have an address. This is represented as an object class in Figure 3.1 by an object class student with identifier stuNo, and attributes name and address. The "?" indicates that the attribute address is optional.*

Relationship Type

Two object classes are connected via a relationship type. A relationship type in the ORA-SS data model represents a nesting relationship. Each relationship type has a degree and participation constraints. A relationship type of degree 2 (i.e. a binary relationship type) relates two object classes. One object class is the parent and the other the child, and we distinguish between the participation constraint on the parent in the relationship type and the participation constraint on the child in the relationship type. A relationship type of degree 3 (i.e. a ternary relationship) is a relationship type among three object classes.

In an ORA-SS schema diagram, a solid labeled directed edge connecting object classes represents a relationship type. A relationship type has a label of the form *name(object class list), n, a : b, c : d*. The label indicates a relationship type with name *name,* among objects in the *object class list* of degree n ($n = 2$ indicates binary, $n = 3$ indicates ternary, etc.), where the participation of the parent has minimum a and maximum b, and the participation of the child has minimum c and maximum d. The *name* is optional. The *object class list* is included only if the object classes participating in the relationship type are separated by some other object class(es) not relevant to the relationship type in

the path that contains all the participating object classes. By defining participation constraints with min:max notation, we are able to represent numerical
constraints. The usual shorthand can also be used to represent the participation
constraints, ? represents $0:1$, * represents $0:n$, + represents $1:n$. All
fields in the label are optional. There is no default value for name. The default
degree is 2, default parent participation constraint is $0:m$, and default child
participation constraint is $1:n$.

Example 3.2 *The ORA-SS schema diagram in Figure 3.2(a) shows a binary
relationship type, jm, between project and member and a binary relationship
type, mp, between member and publication.*

*The relationship type between project and member is annotated with the
label jm, 2, +, +, which represents a many-to-many binary relationship type
between project and member, and a total participation constraint on both
object classes. That is, each project has at least one member, and each member must participate in at least one project. The relationship type between
member and publication is a many-to-many binary relationship type. However a member has zero to many publications, and each publication must
belong to at least one member.*

*Figure 3.2(b) depicts an instance of this schema showing a relationship
type between projects and members, and another between members and
publications, but no relationship type between projects and publications.
This diagram indicates that member m1 has publications pub1, pub2 and
pub3, and m1 works on projects p1 and p3. However, we do not know which
project the publications are associated with. The DataGuide in Figure 3.2(c)
illustrates how these relationships would typically be nested.*

Example 3.3 *In contrast, the ORA-SS schema diagram in Figure 3.3(a) shows
a ternary relationship type between project, member and publication, representing the publications a member has for a particular project. There is a
binary relationship type (named jm) between project and member, and a
relationship type (named Jmp) among project, member and publication.*

*Figure 3.3(b) depicts an instance of this schema, showing a relationship
type between project and member, and another relationship type between the
project and member relationship type and publications. It is clear that publications pub1 and pub2 are associated with member m1 working on project
p1, while publication pub3 is associated with member m1 working on project
p3. The DataGuide in Figure 3.3(c) illustrates how these relationships would
typically be nested.*

Note that the schema diagrams in Figure 3.2(a) and Figure 3.3(a) capture
different semantic information. Figure 3.2(a) captures information about who

40

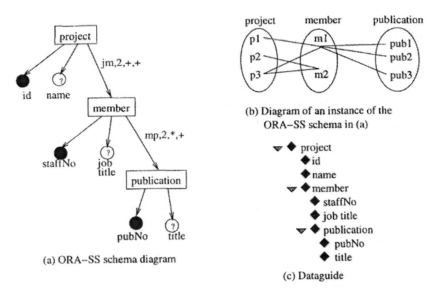

(a) ORA–SS schema diagram

(b) Diagram of an instance of the ORA–SS schema in (a)

(c) Dataguide

Figure 3.2. Representing binary relationship types in an ORA-SS Schema Diagram

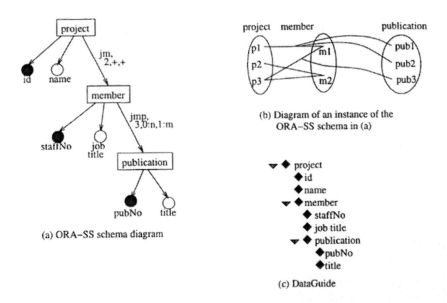

(a) ORA–SS schema diagram

(b) Diagram of an instance of the ORA–SS schema in (a)

(c) DataGuide

Figure 3.3. Representing ternary relationship types in an ORA-SS Schema Diagram

works on what project and information about what publications each person has, while Figure 3.3(a) captures information about who works on what project and information about what publications each person has for a given project.

This distinction between binary and ternary relationships is important for interpreting the meaning of the data and necessary because the degree of a relationship will affect the way the data is stored in a repository. If a ternary relationship is stored as two binary relationships then information is lost. Notice that the DataGuide representations in Figures 3.2(c) and 3.3(c) are the same, because the DataGuide diagram does not express the degree of a relationship type. Although the diagram instances in Figure 3.2(b) and Figure 3.3(b) are different, two XML documents that represent the data instances are exactly the same. This is because it is not possible to express the degree of a relationship type in XML.

Example 3.4 *Let us consider how the relationship types represented in Figure 3.2(a) can be stored in a nested relational database. We would create a relation for each object class and a relation for each relationship type. One relationship type relation stores the project id and the member staffNo, representing the relationship type between object classes project and member, and the other relation stores the member staffNo and the publication pubNo, representing the relationship type between object classes member and publication. The relations are:*

> *Object class relations:*
>   *project(id,name)*   *id is the key*
>   *member(staffNo, jobtitle)*   *staffNo is the key*
>   *publication(pubNo, title)*   *pubNo is the key*
>
> *Relationship type relations:*
>   *jm(id, staffNo)*   *id, staffNo form the key*
>   *mp(staffNo, pubNo)*   *staffNo, pubNo form the key*

On the other hand, for the schema represented in Figure 3.3(a), we would create one relationship type relation that stores the project id, member staffNo and the publication pubNo representing the relationship type among object classes project, member and publication. The object class relations would remain the same as above, and there would be only one relationship type relation:

> *jmp(id, staffNo, pubNo)*   *id, staffNo, pubNo form the key*

As we can see from the examples, the nested relational schema is different for the different meanings, although the same DataGuide is used to model the different semantics in the semistructured data model.

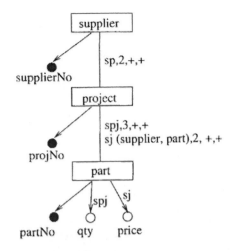

Figure 3.4. Representing a binary and ternary relationship type in an ORA-SS Schema Diagram

   Although the *object class list* is not usually needed in the relationship type label, it is needed when the object classes participating in a relationship type are separated by other object classes not participating in the relationship type in an ORA-SS schema diagram. The following example demonstrates a case where the object class list is needed.

Example 3.5 *Consider three object classes supplier, project, and part, where projects belong to suppliers and parts are supplied for projects. We may also want to represent a relationship type between supplier, and part, particularly if the relationship type between supplier and part has its own properties. These relationship types are shown in Figure 3.4.*
   The relationship type sp is a binary relationship type between supplier and project. The relationship type spj is a ternary relationship type among supplier, project, and part, and the relationship type sj is a binary relationship type between supplier and part.
   Attribute qty is an attribute of relationship type spj, and attribute price is an attribute of sj. Attribute qty represents the quantity of parts supplied to a project by a supplier, and attribute price represents the price of a part from a supplier.

   Just as in traditional data modeling, the concept of identifier is important when data storage structures are being designed. In traditional data modeling, the uniqueness of the identifier represents "real world" uniqueness. This concept of uniqueness is different from the uniqueness of an ID attribute in DTDs, which represents the uniqueness of an attribute within an XML document. For example, a *project* has a unique *projNo* in the real world. However, the same *project* (with the same *projNo*) can be associated with more than one *supplier*, and can appear more than once in an XML document. In a DTD, the *projNo* cannot be declared as an ID attribute in the *project* element. In ORA-SS schema diagrams, the concept of identifier is similar to the meaning in the object oriented data model.

Identifier Dependency Relationship Type

Further, some object classes may not have unique identifiers. For example, while a chapter number is unique within a book, it is not a unique identifier amongst chapters of more than one book, and thus, it cannot be an identifier. To illustrate this point, consider the case where someone refers to chapter 1. It is not obvious which chapter 1 they are referring to. However, if they refer to ISBN 0-07-232206-3, chapter 1, then they uniquely identify a chapter in a particular book. This concept was identified in XML by [Buneman et al., 2001b], and is similar to the concepts of weak identifier and weak entity type of an identifier dependency relationship type in an ER diagram. Some elements, such as paragraphs within a chapter, have no identifier at all.

Identifier dependency relationship types are represented in ORA-SS schema diagrams by a diamond with a label *IDD*. The child in an identifier dependency relationship type is called the *dependent object class*. The identifying attribute(s) in the dependent object class forms a weak identifier, and is depicted in the ORA-SS schema diagram as an attribute with a line through its incoming edge.

Example 3.6 *In Figure 3.5, the object class book has an identifier isbn, while object class paragraph has no identifier. Instances of object class chapter can be identified using the isbn value of the book and the value of the weak identifier chapter number of the chapter. Object class chapter is a dependent object class.*

Attribute

Attributes represent properties, and can be a property of an object class or a property of a relationship type. In an ORA-SS diagram, an attribute is a labeled circle. The label inside the circle shows the cardinality of the attribute. The cardinality is represented using the symbols ? representing an optional single valued attribute, + representing a mandatory multi valued attribute, * representing an optional multi-valued attribute, and the default is a mandatory single valued attribute. The label outside the circle is of the form *name, F* : $v_1, D : v_2$ where *name* is the name of the attribute. The labels *F* and *D* denote

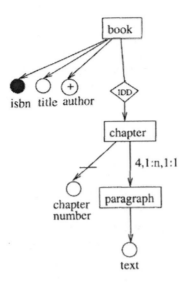

Figure 3.5. Object classes with no identifier or a weak identifier in an ORA-SS Schema Diagram

the *fixed value* and *default value,* and their values are v_1 and v_2 respectively. Both $F : v_1, D : v_2$ are optional.

There is a special name ANY indicating an attribute with unknown structure. This attribute is needed because of the irregularity of semistructured data, and can be used when the structure of some parts of the data are not known or are not of interest.

A filled circle represents an *identifier.* The concept of identifier is borrowed from the object oriented model, where an identifier value can identify an object. A filled circle with a circle around it represents a *candidate identifier.*

The attributes participating in a *composite identifier* or a *composite candidate identifier* are represented by filled circles and their incoming edges are connected with a line. A *derived attribute* is represented by a dashed circle. The edge between an object class and an attribute can be labeled with *name.* The name must be the name of a relationship type, indicating that the attribute is an attribute of that relationship type. A *composite attribute* is a tree of attributes.

Example 3.7 *Consider the ORA-SS schema diagram in Figure 3.6. The object class course has attributes code, title, an attribute whose structure is unknown, currency and cost. Attribute code is the identifier of course and is a composite attribute. It is made up of the attributes dept prefix and number. The default value of dept prefix is comp, denoted as D : comp. An attribute like title is a mandatory single valued attribute so every course is expected to have a value for title. Attribute cost is an optional single valued attribute*

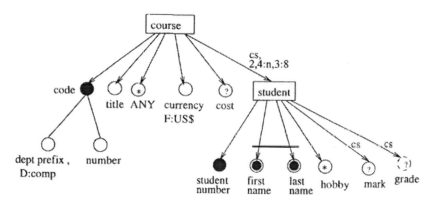

Figure 3.6. Object classes with relationship types and attributes in an ORA-SS Schema Diagram

so not every course is expected to have a value for cost. Attribute currency has a fixed value, US$, for all instances of course. Attribute ANY can contain anything, it is an attribute whose structure is unknown. There is a binary relationship type cs between object classes course and student.

The object class student has an identifier student number, a composite candidate identifier consisting of the attributes first name and last name, and a multi-valued attribute hobby. The attribute mark belongs to the relationship type cs between course and student, i.e. it is the mark for a student in a course. Attribute grade is a derived attribute that belongs to relationship type cs. This is because the value of grade can be calculated from the student's mark in the course.

An identifier is unique amongst the instances of an object class, and represents "real world" uniqueness, rather than uniqueness amongst a set of instances in a nested relationship. For example, while a chapter number is unique within a book, it is not a unique identifier amongst all instances of chapter, so cannot be an identifier. However, student number does uniquely identify students, so even when the *student* object class is nested within the *course* object class, attribute *student number* is still the identifier of object class *student*. The notion of an identifier of an object class differs from the ID attribute in the DTD language, which specifies uniqueness within an XML document.

We advocate that it is necessary to distinguish between attributes of object classes and attributes of relationship types. The distinction is important when views on underlying data are defined. More details on this can be found in Chapter 6.

46

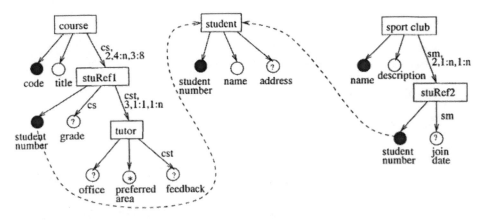

Figure 3.7. Referencing an object class in an ORA-SS Schema Diagram

Reference

A reference usually represents a binary relationship type between two object classes and is used to reduce redundancy. A similar concept is used in the object oriented data model. A reference is denoted by a dashed arrow between a referencing object class and a referenced object class. The referencing and referenced object classes can have different labels and different attributes and relationship types.

Example 3.8 *Consider the ORA-SS schema in Figure 3.7. The object class stuRef1 is a child of object class course, and references object class student which has detailed information about each student. The relationship type cs has attribute grade, and there is a ternary relationship type among object classes course, stuRef1 and tutor. The participation constraints enforce that a tutor tutors at least one student in a course to a maximum of many students in courses, while a student in a course has one and only one tutor. There is an object class sport club that has identifier name and attribute description. The relationship type sm between object classes sport club and stuRef2 has attribute join date. There is a reference between stuRef2 and student.*

A recursive relationship can easily be modeled using references. There is a reference connecting the recursing object class to itself.

Example 3.9 *The schema in Figure 3.8 shows that the prerequisites of a course are other courses. In fact in Figure 3.8, there is a constraint that a course can have 0 to 5 prerequisites, and a prerequisite course can be the prerequisite of 1 or more courses. Object class prerequisite is the referencing object class, and course is the referenced object class.*

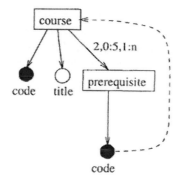

Figure 3.8. Example of a recursive relationship in ORA-SS Schema Diagrams

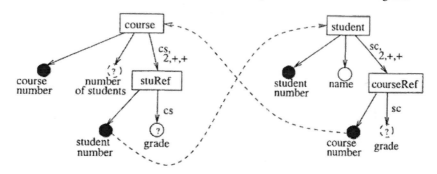

Figure 3.9. Symmetric relationship in an ORA-SS Schema Diagram

Many-to-many relationship types in a tree data structure introduce redundancy, and are not easily modeled. The objective of references is to reduce such redundancy, as shown in the following example.

Example 3.10 *Consider the relationship between courses and students, where a course has students and a student takes courses. If most queries ask about students within courses then it would be practical to have only the reference from stuRef to student. However, if there are also frequent queries about courses that students take, the more general model has a reference between stuRef and student, and another between courseRef and course. Since there is no good reason to nest student within course, or course within student, this many-to-many relationship type is modeled using references in Figure 3.9.*

Notice that both relationship type cs and sc have an attribute grade, representing a student's grade within a course. Attribute grade of relationship type sc is derived from attribute grade of relationship type cs.

Problems, involving the nesting of many-to-many relationships in a hierarchical data model, like that illustrated in Example 3.10 were first encountered in the hierarchical database management system IMS of IBM, where IMS provides physical and virtual pairing to resolve this problem for binary relationship types [Date, 1975]. However, for relationship types of degree n, where $n > 2$, physical and virtual pairings cannot be used to resolve redundancy problems properly.

Ordering

Ordering on elements is assumed in XML documents. However, in the real world, not all entities are ordered and there are different kinds of ordering. We distinguish between 3 kinds of ordering in the ORA-SS data model to provide flexibility when modeling the real world:

1 ordering on instances of an object class in relation to another object class, e.g., ordering on chapters of a book,

2 ordering on values of an attribute, e.g. ordering on authors of a book, and

3 ordering on attributes and object classes of an object class, e.g. ordering on parts of a book, like preface, table of contents, chapters, appendix.

The first kind of ordering is represented by a "<" in the relationship type label, the second is represented by a "<" on the edge to the attribute, while the third is represented by a "<" beside the object class. These symbols are optional and the default is no ordering.

Example 3.11 *Consider the ORA-SS schema diagram in Figure 3.10. The symbol "<" on the edge between object class book and attribute author indicates that the values of the attribute author are ordered. The symbol "<" adjacent to object class book indicates that the attributes and object classes of this object class are ordered i.e. the structure of book is isbn, title, authors, preface, toc, followed by the object class chapter. The symbol "<" in the relationship type label for the IDD relationship type indicates that the instances of object class chapter are ordered. The "<" in the edge between object classes chapter and attribute paragraph indicates that the values of attribute paragraph of a chapter are ordered.*

When XML documents are stored in a repository, it is important to be able to represent and enforce as many of the constraints as is practical. If a data model is being used in the mapping from the XML document to the repository, then it is important that the data model can also model the constraints, such as ordering.

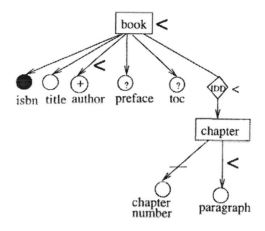

Figure 3.10. Ordered object classes, attributes, and attribute values in an ORA-SS Schema Diagram

Disjunction

A characteristic of semistructured data is that attributes and object classes are likely to be less homogeneous than in structured data. To allow for this, we provide for two different kinds of disjunction in the ORA-SS data model:

1 disjunctive object classes, and

2 disjunctive attributes.

A disjunctive relationship is used to represent disjunctive object classes, such as a student lives in a hostel OR at home, and is represented by a relationship diamond labeled with symbol "|". A disjunctive attribute is represented by a circle labeled with symbol "|", with edges from this circle to the alternatives.

Example 3.12 *Consider the schema diagram in Figure 3.11. A course has a disjunctive attribute exam venue. Attribute exam venue is a disjunctive single-valued attribute, and can be a lecture theatre or a laboratory, but not both. It is denoted by a "|" inside a circle. Relationship sh is a disjunctive relationship, and is denoted by a "|" inside a diamond. It represents the fact that a student can either live in a hostel or at home. The participation constraints indicate that an instance of this relationship is mandatory, and a student must have an address of either a hostel or home.*

3.2   ORA-SS Data Instance Diagram

Traditionally, when databases are designed, the schema is modeled using a conceptual model and the schema of the database is derived from this model.

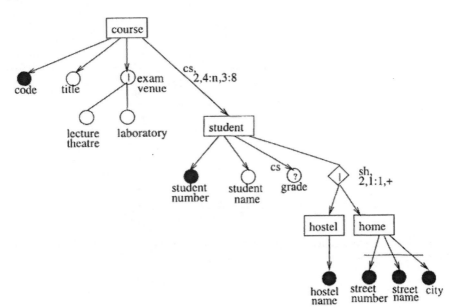

Figure 3.11. Disjunctive attribute and object classes in an ORA-SS Schema Diagram

With semistructured data, the focus is more on the instance and the schema is derived from the instance. The semistructured data instance can be modeled using an ORA-SS instance diagram.

An ORA-SS instance diagram is a directed graph where each internal node is an object (or instance of an object class), and each leaf node is an attribute with value. Each directed edge indicates a relationship between the parent and child nodes. The objects are represented by rectangles with a label *name* inside. The attributes with values are represented by labeled circles. The label of an attribute has the form *name : value* where *name* is the name of the attribute and *value* is the value of the attribute.

Example 3.13 *Consider Figure 3.12, where department, course and student represent object instances, and the label "code : CS1102" on the circle states the name of the attribute is code, and the value of the attribute is CS1102. An XML document representing the information expressed in the ORA-SS instance diagram in Figure 3.12 is shown in Figure 3.13. The schema of the instance is represented in the ORA-SS schema diagram in Figure 3.14, with the corresponding DTD in Figure 3.15.*

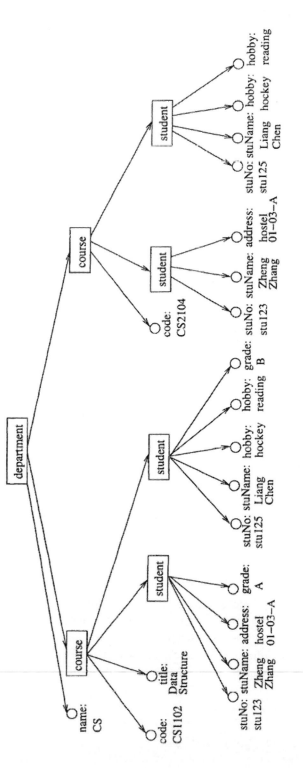

Figure 3.12.   ORA-SS Instance Diagram for document in Figure 2.1

52

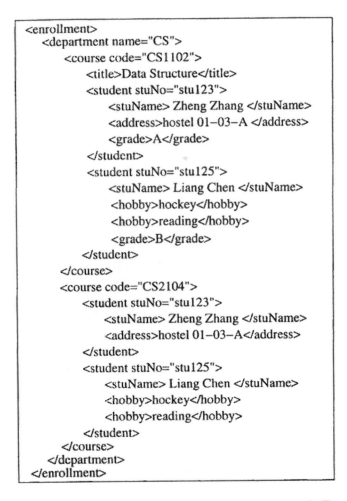

```
<enrollment>
    <department name="CS">
        <course code="CS1102">
            <title>Data Structure</title>
            <student stuNo="stu123">
                <stuName> Zheng Zhang </stuName>
                <address>hostel 01-03-A </address>
                <grade>A</grade>
            </student>
            <student stuNo="stu125">
                <stuName> Liang Chen </stuName>
                <hobby>hockey</hobby>
                <hobby>reading</hobby>
                <grade>B</grade>
            </student>
        </course>
        <course code="CS2104">
            <student stuNo="stu123">
                <stuName> Zheng Zhang </stuName>
                <address>hostel 01-03-A</address>
            </student>
            <student stuNo="stu125">
                <stuName> Liang Chen </stuName>
                <hobby>hockey</hobby>
                <hobby>reading</hobby>
            </student>
        </course>
    </department>
</enrollment>
```

Figure 3.13. An XML Document for the ORA-SS Instance Diagram in Figure 3.12

3.3 ORA-SS Functional Dependency Diagram

Functional dependencies and multivalued dependencies model real world constraints, showing that some of the object classes or attributes depend on other object classes or attributes. There are two kinds of dependency. The first kind has attributes of object classes and relationship types on the righthand side of the dependency. This kind is illustrated in Figure 3.14, where:

$$code \rightarrow title$$
$$stuNo \rightarrow stuName, address$$
$$stuNo \twoheadrightarrow hobby$$

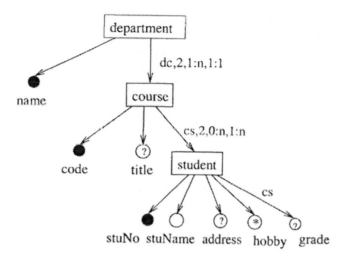

Figure 3.14.   ORA-SS Schema Diagram for document in Figure 3.12

```
<!ELEMENT enrollment    (department+)>
<!ELEMENT department    (course+)>
    <!ATTLIST department  name  ID  #REQUIRED>
<!ELEMENT course    (title?, student*)>
    <!ATTLIST course  code  ID   #REQUIRED>
<!ELEMENT title    (#PCDATA)>
<!ELEMENT student    (stuName, address?, hobby*, grade?)>
    <!ATTLIST student  stuNo  #REQUIRED>
<!ELEMENT stuName    (#PCDATA)>
<!ELEMENT address (#PCDATA)>
<!ELEMENT hobby  (#PCDATA)>
<!ELEMENT grade  (#PCDATA)>
```

Figure 3.15.   An DTD for the ORA-SS Schema Diagram in Figure 3.14

$$code, stuNo \rightarrow grade$$

Notice that the DTD in Figure 3.15 cannot fully represent the semantic constraints in the ORA-SS schema diagram in Figure 3.14, such as

$$code, stuNo \rightarrow grade$$

The second kind of dependency involves object classes that are participating in
a relationship type. In Figure 3.14, there is an example:

$$course \rightarrow department$$

This dependency can be derived from the ORA-SS schema diagram but this
kind of dependency cannot always be derived, and needs to be represented in
a separate functional dependency diagram for the relationship type involved.

In general, functional dependencies of binary relationship types can be derived from the participation constraints in the ORA-SS schema diagram, but it may not be possible for n-ary ($n > 2$) relationship types. Functional dependency diagrams can also be used with ORA-SS schema diagrams to capture the same information. This information is useful when attempting to identify redundancy in the repository. However, because functional dependencies of binary relationship types can be derived from the participation constraints of the binary relationship types in the ORA-SS schema diagrams, there is no need to draw functional dependency diagrams for binary relationships.

In functional dependency diagrams the object classes are represented by labeled rectangles, the relationship types by diamonds labeled only with the relationship type name, and the edges carry the cardinality of the object classes. Each edge label has $c_1 / \ldots / c_m$ where m is the number of functional dependencies among the object classes. The c_1's on each edge emanating from a relationship type relate to each other and represent one functional dependency, as do the c_2's, etc. Each c_i represents the object classes cardinality in that functional dependency, and is denoted as $1, n,$ or $-$.

Consider a ternary relationship among three object classes, A, B and C. If the c_1's are $n, n, 1$ respectively, then we can derive the functional dependency $A, B \rightarrow C$. In fact, an object class with cardinality 1 will appear on the right hand side of the functional dependency, except in the case where all object classes have cardinality 1. In this case, any of the object classes can appear on the right hand side of the functional dependency. A hyphen ("-") indicates that the object class does not take part in the dependency.

Example 3.14 *The functional dependency diagram in Figure 3.16 enhances the information in Figure 3.7. Suppose that a tutor can teach many tutorials in one course, each student in a course has one tutor, and a tutor can teach tutorials in only one course. The functional dependencies that model these constraints are:*

$$student, course \rightarrow tutor$$
$$tutor \rightarrow course.$$

The first functional dependency can be derived from Figure 3.7, but the second cannot. The functional dependencies among the object classes student, course, and tutor are shown on the edges in Figure 3.16. The edge from student has the label $n/-$, the edge from course has the label $n/1$, and the edge from tutor has the label $1/n$. Consider the first character in each label, n, n and 1 respectively, they indicate that for each student and each course, there is at most one tutor, and from this we can derive the functional depen-

dency:

$$student, course \rightarrow tutor.$$

Consider the second character in each label, -, 1, and n respectively, they in-dicate that object class student is not involved in the functional dependency, and for each tutor there is at most one course. From this we can derive the functional dependency:

$$tutor \rightarrow course.$$

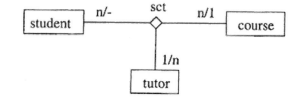

Figure 3.16. Functional dependency diagram enhancing the information in Figure 3.7

There are two advantages in having separate functional dependency dia-grams: the functional dependency diagram may enhance the semantic informa-tion captured in an ORA-SS schema diagram, and some semantic information that can be expressed in an ORA-SS schema diagram can be represented in a functional dependency diagram to separate the concepts.

3.4   ORA-SS Inheritance Hierarchy Diagram

Inheritance is one of the important features of the object oriented model allowing us to represent common properties of object classes. When an ob-ject class O_1 is a subclass of another object class O_2, then O_1 will inherit the properties of O_2. For example, an inheritance hierarchy can be used to show that student is a subclass of person. Such subclass/superclass relationships are represented in an inheritance hierarchy (class hierarchy) diagram in the object oriented model.

The ORA-SS data model also has a similar inheritance hierarchy diagram. The inheritance hierarchy is helpful when organizing data storage, because there are various standard methods of efficiently storing objects that are gen-eralizations/specializations of other objects , like in the object oriented model. Although the methods may not apply directly for semistructured data, we be-lieve they can be modified to fit.

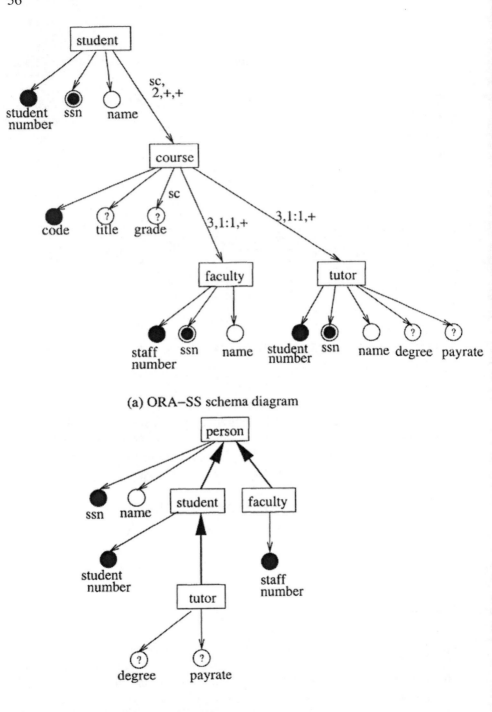

(a) ORA–SS schema diagram

(b) Inheritance diagram

Figure 3.17. ORA-SS Schema Diagram and Inheritance Diagram

Example 3.15 *Consider the ORA-SS schema diagram in Figure 3.17(a). The object classes student, faculty and tutor all have the attributes ssn and name, and that object classes student and tutor both have the attribute student number. The inheritance information is drawn on a separate inheritance diagram. The inheritance information for the object classes in Figure 3.17(a) is recorded in the inheritance diagram in Figure 3.17(b), tutor is a subclass of student and it inherits attributes ssn, name and student number from student which in turn inherits from person. Object classes student and faculty both inherit ssn and name from person. Attribute student number is the identifier of student, and tutor, and staff number is the identifier of faculty. Attribute ssn is their candidate identifier. Notice that rather than replace Figure 3.17(a), Figure 3.17(b) enhances it.*

In fact one object class may be a subclass of two or more superclasses. For such multiple inheritance cases, conflicts may occur where an object class could inherit the same property name from more than one superclass. This is called a multiple inheritance conflict. Methods to describe such conflicts are described in [Ling and Teo, 1993].

3.5   Discussion

The ORA-SS data model is designed specifically for modeling semistructued data. The model consists of four diagrams:

1 ORA-SS schema diagram,

2 ORA-SS instance diagram,

3 ORA-SS functional dependency diagram, and

4 ORA-SS inheritance hierarchy diagram.

In the ORA-SS data model there is a clear distinction between object classes and attributes, which are modeled as rectangles and circles respectively in each of the four diagrams. The major strengths of the ORA-SS data model are that it can model concepts central to the semistructured data model, such as references, ordering on object classes and attributes, and document instances, as well as concepts that have proven important in traditional data modeling, such as binary and n-ary ($n > 2$) relationships, participation constraints on all object classes participating in a relationship type, the inheritance hierarchy between object classes, and the ability to distinguish between attributes of relationship types and attributes of object classes.

Many of the other data models proposed to model semistructured data are based on the DTD language, and as a consequence are unable to model some of the concepts that have been identified as important for modeling data.

This page intentionally left blank

Chapter 4

SCHEMA EXTRACTION

Unlike data stored in traditional relational or object-oriented databases, semistructured data does not have a fixed schema that is known in advance and that can be stored separately from the data. In fact, the structure of semistructured data is irregular, unknown, and changes often [Suciu, 1998].

The lack of external schema information renders the storage, indexing, and querying of semistructured data inefficient, or even impossible. This leads to the development of methods such as DataGuide [Goldman and Widom, 1997] to extract the schema from semistructured data. The focus of these techniques is to extract the hierarchy structure of semistructured data. In contrast, ORA-SS is able to capture important semantic information such as objects classes, relationship types, attributes, degree of relationship types, participation constraints of the object classes in the relationship types. Further, ORA-SS is able to distinguish between attributes of object classes and attributes of relationship types. The ability to extract these semantics from the underlying data will greatly facilitate the various stages of database design and usage.

Consider the attributes *stuName* and *grade* located below the object class *student* in the ORA-SS schema in Figure 4.1. The attribute *stuName* is an attribute of the object class *student* while the attribute *grade* belongs to the relationship type *cs* which involves the object classes *course* and *student*. Therefore, instead of simply storing *grade* with the attributes of *student*, we should store *grade* together with the identifiers of the object classes *student* and *course*.

Such semantic information also alerts us to the fact that any view containing only course and grade information will not be meaningful because we should not omit the student information when considering the attribute *grade*.

In the rest of the chapter, we will present a set of schema extraction rules and a method to extract semantically rich ORA-SS schemas from XML documents.

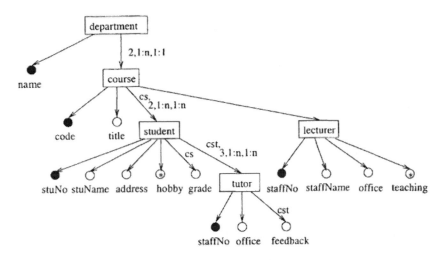

Figure 4.1. Example ORA-SS schema

We will illustrate the schema extraction algorithm with an example and finally compare the proposed approach with existing schema extraction methods.

4.1 Basic Extraction Rules

Before we can extract the schema from an XML document, we must have some knowledge of the structure and syntax of the document. We propose three rules that are based on the XML syntax to guide our schema extraction process.

Rule E1. *The XML document root element is considered as an unique entry into the XML schema. A non-root XML element is classified as*

1 *an* **object** *if it has at least one attribute.*

2 *a* **simple attribute** *if it has only text content without attributes or subelements.*

3 *a* **composite attribute** *if it comprises of multiple subelements whose values are text.*

   A simple or composite attribute is **single-valued** *if the XML element is not repeated under its parent XML element, otherwise, it is a* **multivalued** *attribute.*

This rule can be used to differentiate objects and attributes when they are both expressed by XML elements. Consider the following segment of XML document:

$$< VCD \quad name = \text{``Toy Story''} >$$
$$< price > \$19.95 < /price >$$
$$< quantity > 20 < /quantity >$$
$$< actor > Don \ Rickles < /actor >$$
$$< actor > Kelsey \ Grammer < /actor >$$
$$< actor > Tim \ Allen < /actor >$$
$$< features >$$
$$< media > DVD - R < /media >$$
$$< format > DVD - MP3 < /format >$$
$$< /features >$$
$$< /VCD >$$

VCD is an object since it contains attributes and subelements, while *price* and *quantity* are simple single-valued attributes since they only have text content without any attribute or subelement. The element *actor* is a simple multi-valued attribute as it occurs multiple times under the same parent *VCD* element in the XML document. The *element features* is a composite attribute consisting of the attributes *media* and *format*.

Rule E1 will greatly reduce the number of XML elements that will be considered as objects. This in turn helps to simplify the schema extraction process.

Rule E2. *XML elements permit a mixture of text and elements. We convert the text segment into a subelement by adding some pseudo tag.*

For example, although the following segment is legal in XML, it cannot be captured in semistructured data models.

$$< talk > Learn \ Java \ in \ 20 \ Days$$
$$< speaker > Phil \ Wadler < /speaker >$$
$$< /talk >$$

However, if we add a pseudo tag "title" for the text segment, then the above segment can be converted to

$$< talk >$$
$$< title > Learn \ Java \ in \ 20 \ Days < /title >$$
$$< speaker > Phil \ Wadler < /speaker >$$
$$< /talk >$$

Rule E3. *The attributes of XML elements may be single-valued attributes, identifiers of object classes or IDREF(s). Attributes that are written as subele-*

ments may be attributes of object classes or attributes of relationship types.

XML is ambiguous in the usage of attributes or subelements. One can use the attributes of an XML element or the subelements of an XML element to express the properties of an object class. Rule E3 allows us to determine the attributes of object classes.

For example, in the following XML segment, it is clear that *stuName* and *age* are attributes of the object class *student,* while *grade* may be either an attribute of *student,* or an attribute of a relationship type involving the object classes *course* and *student.*

$$< course \quad code = ``CS1102" \quad title = ``Data \; Structure" >$$
$$< student \quad stuName = ``Benjamin \; Tan" \quad age = ``22" >$$
$$< grade > B+ < /grade >$$
$$< /student >$$
$$< /course >$$

Note that Rule E1, E2, and E3 are heuristic rules to facilitate the schema extraction process. Further, it is easy to convert XML documents to conform to these rules.

4.2 Schema Extraction Algorithm

Based on the above three rules, we are now ready to introduce an ORA-SS schema extraction algorithm. There are two main steps:

1 Generate an initial rough ORA-SS schema structure from the XML document.

2 Refine the rough ORA-SS schema structure by deriving some semantic information from the underlying data.

The refinement of the schema structure may require user verification. This is because, without user input, it is impossible for the algorithm to derive relationship types and their properties such as degree, and participation constraints. It is also not trivial to figure out whether an attribute belongs to an object class or a relationship type. Such information is not available explicitly in the XML documents. However, the algorithm can look for conflicts in the data instances and deduce information such as an attribute cannot be an identifier of an object class.

The final ORA-SS schema will capture the identifiers of object classes, the degrees and participation constraints of relationship types, and information such as whether an attribute belongs to an object class or a relationship type, and whether an attribute is an IDREF(s) to some object class.

The following gives an outline of the schema extraction algorithm.

Algorithm Extract Schema

Step 1. Generate an initial rough ORA-SS schema structure.

(a) Use Rule E2 to convert XML elements that has text mixed with subelements.

(b) Use Rule E1 to identify XML elements that denote object classes and attributes such as multivalued attributes, composite attributes, etc.

Step 2. Refine the rough ORA-SS schema structure with semantic information derived from the data and/or user.

(a) Create a table for each object class, where the columns consist of the attributes of the object class, and rows are the object instances.

(b) Determine the identifier for each object class.

(c) Determine whether an attribute is an IDREF(s) to some object class.

(d) Use Rule E3 to determine whether an attribute is an object attribute.

(e) Discover relationship types, their degree, participation constraints, and attributes.
Create a table for each relationship type.
end

We will now discuss the details of the extraction algorithm.

Step 1. Generate Initial Schema.

Step 1 of the schema extraction algorithm first utilizes Rule E2 to convert a text segment into a subelement. Next, Rule E1 is used to identify the XML elements that depict object classes and attributes. Note that the root element in the XML document is not extracted as an object class since its role is to identify the XML document.

Step 2. Refine Schema.

(a) Create tables for object classes.

The algorithm creates a table for each object class, where the table name and the object class name are the same as the XML element tag name. The columns of the table consist of the attributes of the object class, and rows are the object instances. For a start, all the attributes of the XML element are considered as the object class's attributes. However, we add a mark "?" for attributes which originate from XML subelements, since these may possibly be relationship attributes.

Single-valued composite attributes are represented by their component attributes. A simple multivalued attribute such as X, which has been identified by Rule El, is denoted as $X*(?)$. The value of this column for a tuple is the set of subelement X values under the parent element (i.e., an element which represents an identifier of the object class).

Similarly, multiple composite attributes are represented as a nested table in the object class relation with all the component attributes as the attributes of the nested table.

(b) Determine identifier of object classes.

In order to determine the identifier of each object class, the algorithm will analyze the single-valued attribute values of each object class.

A single-valued attribute is a possible object class identifier if each of its attribute values determines a unique value for the other attributes which have not been marked with a "?" in the object class table.

The user will be asked to verify the identifier of the object class. We observe that the identifier is typically the first attribute in the XML element attribute list. Note that attributes that contain null values cannot be an identifier.

(c) Determine IDREF(S).

The algorithm will also determine whether an attribute is a potential IDREF(S) to some object class. An IDREF consists of only one value, while an IDREFS comprises of values that are separated by blanks. Since the identifier of an object class cannot be also an IDREF to other object class, the algorithm will analyze the non-identifier single-valued attribute of each object class, and check whether all its values appear as identifier values of some object class.

Further, if the algorithm finds blank characters in an attribute value, then it will tokenize the value to become a set of values, using the blank as the separator. If all the tokenized values correspond to the values of identifier value of some object class, then this attribute is a potential IDREFS. Note that the same object class can be involved, in which case, this IDEREF(S) represents a recursive relationship type. The algorithm will seek user verification before setting the attribute to be an IDREFS to that object class. In this way, the reference will be restricted to a certain object class, which is more meaningful in real world.

(d) Determine attributes of object classes.

Next, we want to examine whether an attribute belongs to an object class. From Rule E3, attributes that originate from the attributes of an XML element are definitely attributes of an object class. However, attributes that originate from XML subelements can be either an attribute of an object class or a relationship type.

The algorithm checks whether the values of a single-valued attribute or sets of values of a multivalued attribute that originate from XML subelements can be determined by the identifier values of the object class. If yes, then the user is asked to verify that the attribute is indeed an object class attribute. Otherwise, the attribute is not an attribute of the object class and the corresponding column will be removed from the object class's table. Any resulting identical rows in the object table will be merged. The column will be subsequently added to the appropriate relationship table.

(e) Determine relationship types and their properties.

A relationship type exists between the object classes that occurs in a path from the root to leaf in the initial rough schema. Hence, for each root-to-leaf path in the initial schema, we create a relationship type table that comprises of the identifiers of the object classes that occur in the path. Further, if the lowest object class in the path has attributes that have not been identified as object class attributes, and are still marked with a "?", then these attributes are also inserted into the relationship type table. Note that composite and multivalued attributes are handled similarly as in the object tables.

Additionally, we create a relationship type table for each remaining attribute that has not been identified as an object class attribute, and is still marked with a "?". The columns of such tables consist of the attribute, and the identifiers of object classes from the root to the object class which the attribute is connected to.

Next, the algorithm tries to determine the minimal possible degree of each relationship type. The schema tree is traversed in a bottom-up manner to check whether a relationship type can be a binary one. This is achieved by examining the values of the last two objects' identifiers. If both identifiers have the same values, but differ from the relationship attribute value (or set of the relationship attribute values if it is a multivalued attribute), then this relationship type is not a binary relationship.

Otherwise, the algorithm checks whether the relationship type is ternary, quadruple, etc. This approach enables us to find the minimal possible degree of the relationship type based on the current set of data. Note that we will still seek user verification, who is allowed to set a higher degree for the relationship type. The user will also be asked to name each relationship type.

After determining the degree of each relationship type, the algorithm will update the relationship table accordingly. The identifier columns of object classes which do not participate in the relationship type will be deleted, and any resulting identical rows will be merged. Further, if two or more relationship attributes belong to the same relationship type, they will be merged into the same relationship table.

For each relationship table, the algorithm will count the number of identifier values and generate the minimal possible range of participation constraints, according to the data in the corresponding relationship table. Again, the user can override and set the participation constraints to be at a wider range, e.g. 2:5 can be set to 1:10, or 1:n, or *, +, etc.

The algorithm will also check that the final ORA-SS schema obtained is consistent with the XML document.

4.3 Example

We use the following XML document to illustrate how the schema extraction algorithm works.

$< ?xml\ version = "1.0"? >$

$< enrollment >$
$\quad < course\ code = "CS1102"\ title = "Data\ Structure" >$
$\qquad < student\ stuNo = "stu123"\ stuName = "Zheng\ Zhang"$
$\qquad\qquad address = "hostel\ 01 - 03 - A" >$

$\qquad\qquad < grade > A < /grade >$
$\qquad\qquad < tutor\ staffNo = "stf101"\ office = "S17 - 05 - 07" >$
$\qquad\qquad\qquad < feedback > very\ interesting\ course < /feedback >$
$\qquad\qquad < /tutor >$
$\qquad < /student >$

$\qquad < student\ stuNo = "stu125"\ stuName = "Liang\ Chen"$
$\qquad\qquad address = "hostel\ 01 - 04 - C" >$

$\qquad\qquad < hobby > hockey < /hobby >$
$\qquad\qquad < hobby > reading < /hobby >$
$\qquad\qquad < grade > B < /grade >$

```
< tutor  staffNo = "stf101"  office = "S17 − 05 − 07" >
    < feedback > a bit difficult < /feedback >
< /tutor >
< /student >

< student  stuNo = "std126"  stuName = "Xiaochun Wang"
        address − "hostel 02 − 04 − A" >

    < hobby > swimming < /hobby >
    < hobby > tennis < /hobby >
    < grade > A+ < /grade >
    < tutor  staffNo = "stf102"  office = "S15 − 06 − 03" >
        < feedback > learnt a lot in this course < /feedback >
    < /tutor >
< /student >

< student  stuNo = "std130"  stuName = "Mingming Liu"
        address = "hostel 03 − 01 − F" >

    < grade > B+ < /grade >
    < tutor  staffNo = "stf102"  office = "S15 − 06 − 03" >
        < feedback > boring < /feedback >
    < /tutor >
< /student >

< lecturer  staffNo = "stf001"  staffName = "Jie Xu"
        office = "S17 − 04 − 25"  teaching = "CS1102" >
< /lecturer >
< /course >

< course  code = "CS2104"  title = "Programming Concepts" >
    < student  stuNo = "stu123"  stuName = "Zheng Zhang"
            address = "hostel 01 − 03 − A" >

        < grade > B < /grade >
        < tutor  staffNo = "stf101"  office = "S17 − 05 − 07" >
            < feedback > approachable tutor < /feedback >
        < /tutor >
    < /student >

    < student  stuNo = "stu125"  stuName = "Liang Chen"
            address = "hostel 01 − 04 − C" >

        < hobby > hockey < /hobby >
        < hobby > reading < /hobby >
        < grade > A < /grade >
        < tutor  staffNo = "stf101"  office = "S17 − 05 − 07" >
            < feedback > friendly and approachable < /feedback >
        < /tutor >
    < /student >
```

$$< student \; stuNo = "std126" \; stuName = "Xiaochun \; Wang"$$
$$address = "hostel \; 02 - 04 - A" >$$

$$< hobby > swimming < /hobby >$$
$$< hobby > tennis < /hobby >$$
$$< grade > B- < /grade >$$
$$< tutor \; staffNo = "stf101" \; office = "S17 - 05 - 07" >$$
$$< feedback > helpful < /feedback >$$
$$< /tutor >$$
$$< /student >$$

$$< lecturer \; staffNo = "stf002" \; staffName = "Dachuan \; Zhou"$$
$$office = "S15 - 03 - 15" \; teaching = "CS1102 \; CS2104" / >$$

$$< /course >$$
$$< /enrollment >$$

Step 1. Generate Initial Schema.

The algorithm first uses Rule E1 to determine the object classes *course* *student, tutor* and *lecturer* together with their attributes and subelements. An initial rough ORA-SS schema tree as shown in Figure 4.2 is obtained. Note that the root element of the XML document, that is, *enrollment* is not mapped to an object class since it is just an identifier of the XML document.

The symbol "?" on the edge between an object and an attribute indicates that we have yet to determine whether the attribute is an object attribute or a relationship attribute.

Step 2. Refine Initial Schema.

(a) Create tables for object classes.

Next, the algorithm will refine the initial schema structure with the semantic information obtained from the underlying XML document. User verification is needed at this step.

The algorithm will create a table for each object class. Table 4.1 shows the tables for all the object classes *course, lecturer, student* and *tutor*. These tables are populated with data from the XML document. The values of each XML element are mapped to the corresponding column in the table.

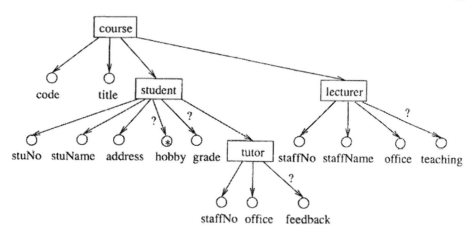

Figure 4.2. Initial ORA-SS schema structure after Step 1

(b) Determine identifiers of object classes.

Next, the algorithm will analyze the instances in the object class tables to determine the identifier for the object classes. We can use any data mining technique to mine possible functional dependencies among the attributes in the object tables. Attributes that are marked with "?" are excluded here.

From the instances in the object class *course* table (Table 4.1), we have the functional dependencies

$$code \rightarrow title$$
$$title \rightarrow code$$

This implies that both *code* and *title* are candidate keys of *course*. Since *code* is the first attribute, the algorithm will first ask the user if *code* is the identifier of the object class *course*. If it is not, then the algorithm will proceed to ask the user whether *title* is the identifier of *course*.

For the object class *lecturer*, we have the functional dependency

$$staffNo \rightarrow staffName, office, teaching$$

Thus, the algorithm will ask the user to verify that *staffNo* is the identifier of the object class *lecturer*

From the instances in the object class *student*, we have the functional dependency

Table 4.1. Object class tables *course, lecturer, student* and *tutor*

table: course

code	title
CS1102	Data Structure
CS2104	Programming Concepts

table: student

stuNo	stuName	address	hobby * (?)	grade (?)
stu123	Zheng Zhang	hostel 01-03-A		A
stu125	Liang Chen	hostel 01-04-C	{hockey; reading}	B
stu126	Xiaochun Wang	hostel 02-04-A	{swimming; tennis}	A+
stu130	Mingming Liu	hostel 03-01-F		B+
stu123	Zheng Zhang	hostel 01-03-A		B
stu125	Liang Chen	hostel 01-04-C	{hockey; reading}	A
stu126	Xiaochun Wang	hostel 02-04-A	{swimming; tennis}	B-

table: tutor

staffNo	office	feedback (?)
stf101	S17-05-07	very interesting course
stf101	S17-05-07	a bit difficult
stf101	S17-05-07	approachable tutor
stf101	S17-05-07	approachable and friendly
stf101	S17-05-07	helpful
stf102	S15-06-03	learnt a lot in this course
stf102	S15-06-03	boring

table: lecturer

staffNo	staffName	office	teaching (?)	
stf001	Jie Xu	S17-04-25	CS1102	
stf002	Dachuan Zhou	S15-03-15	CS1102	CS2104

$$stuNo \rightarrow stuName, address$$

The user is asked whether *stuNo* is the identifier of the object class *student*. If the answer is affirmative, then *stuNo* is set to be the identifier of *student*. Similarly, we have *staffNo* as an identifier of *tutor*.

(c) Determine IDREF(S).

The extraction algorithm tries to check whether some attribute is an IDREF or IDREFS to some object class. Since all the values of the attribute *teaching,*

Table 4.2. Final object class tables *student* and *tutor*

table: course *identifier: code*

code	title
CS1102	Data Structure
CS2104	Programming Concepts

table: student *identifier: stuNo*

stuNo	stuName	address	hobby*
stu123	Zheng Zhang	hostel 01-03-A	
stu125	Liang Chen	hostel 01-04-C	{hockey; reading}
stu126	Xiaochun Wang	hostel 02-04-A	{swimming; tennis}
stu130	Mingming Liu	hostel 03-01-F	

table: tutor *identifier: staffNo*

staffNo	office
stf101	S17-05-07
stf102	S15-06-03

table: lecturer *identifier: staffNo*

staffNo	staffName	office	teaching*
stf001	Jie Xu	S17-04-25	{CS1102}
stf002	Dachuan Zhou	S15-03-15	{CS1102; CS2104}

that is, *CS1102* and *CS2104* after tokenization, form a subset of the values of the object identifier / candidate key *code* of the object class *course*, it is highly likely that *teaching* is an IDREF to the object class *course*. This observation is highlighted to the user who confirms that *teaching* is an IDREF to the object class *course*.

(d) Determine attributes of object classes.

This step examines whether the attributes that are marked with "?" are attributes of object classes. Since each student in Table 4.1 has a unique set of hobby values, the user is asked whether *hobby* is a multivalued attribute of *student*. If it is, then we mark the attribute *hobby* with an "*".

The functional dependency

$$stuNo \rightarrow grade$$

does not hold because student *stu123* has two grade values *A* and *B*. Therefore, *grade* is not an attribute of the *student* object class.

Similarly, the attribute *feedback* is also not an object class attribute.

Table 4.3. Relationship type tables cst and cl

table: cst   *identifier: {code, stuNo, staffNo}*

code	stuNo	tutor.staffNo	grade	feedback
CS1102	stu123	stf101	A	very interesting course
CS1102	stu125	stf101	B	a bit difficulty
CS1102	stu126	stf102	A+	learnt a lot in this course
CS1102	stu130	stf102	B+	boring
CS2104	stu123	stf101	B	approachable tutor
CS2104	stu125	stf101	A	friendly and approachable
CS2104	stu126	stf101	B-	helpful

table: cl   *identifier: {code, staffNo}*

code	lecturer.staffNo
CS1102	stf001
CS1102	stf002
CS2104	stf002

Since *grade* and *feedback* are not object class attributes, they will be removed from the *student* table and the *tutor* table respectively. Table 4.2 shows the updated tables of the various object classes.

(e) Determine relationship types and their attributes.

Finally, the algorithm determines the various relationship types that exist in the XML document and tries to obtain the minimal possible degrees of these relationships types.

For each root-to-leaf path in the ORA-SS schema, the algorithm creates a relationship table comprising of the identifiers of the object classes that occur in the path (see Table 4.3). Note that the remaining attributes *grade* and *feedback* that are still marked with "?" are placed in the relationship type table *cst*.

From the instances in the XML document, we find that each *grade* value is unique for each pair of *(code, stuNo)* value; and that each *feedback* value is unique for each pair of *(code, stuNo, staffNo)* value. These findings are verified with the user.

Since *grade* is an attribute of the relationship type involving *course* and *student*, we create another relationship table called *cs* involving *code*, *stuNo* and *grade*. The attribute *grade* is removed from the table *cst*. Table 4.4 shows the final set of relationship type tables obtained.

Table 4.4. Final relationship type tables cs, cst and cl

table: cs   identifier: {code, stuNo}

code	stuNo	grade
CS1102	stu123	A
CS1102	stu125	B
CS1102	stu126	A+
CS1102	stu130	B+
CS2104	stu123	B
CS2104	stu125	A
CS2104	stu126	B-

table: cst   identifier: {code, stuNo, staffNo}

code	stuNo	tutor.staffNo	feedback
CS1102	stu123	stf101	very interesting course
CS1102	stu125	stf101	a bit difficult
CS1102	stu126	stf102	learnt a lot in this course
CS1102	stu130	stf102	challenging course
CS2104	stu123	stf101	approachable tutor
CS2104	stu125	stf101	friendly and approachable
CS2104	stu126	stf101	helpful

table: cl   identifier: {code, staffNo}

code	lecturer.staffNo
CS1102	stf001
CS1102	stf002
CS2104	stf002

Based on the data in Table 4.4, the minimal possible parent participation constraint and child participation constraint of the relationship type *cs* could be 3:4 and 1:2 respectively, that is, 3-4 students can be enrolled in a course, and a student can take 1-2 courses.

Similarly, the minimal possible parent *(student)* participation constraint and child *(tutor)* participation constraint of relationship type *cst* could be 1:1 and 2:2 respectively, For the relationship type *cs*, the user is allowed to change the the parent participation constraint to 3:n, where *n* indicates that the maximum occurrences is infinitely many.

The user can also change the child participation constraint to 1:6, that is, a student can take a maximum of 6 courses. The new constraints are super ranges of that discovered by the system.

Figure 4.3 shows the final ORA-SS schema tree extracted from our example XML document. Note that the system should verify that the final ORA-SS schema tree is consistent with the original XML document.

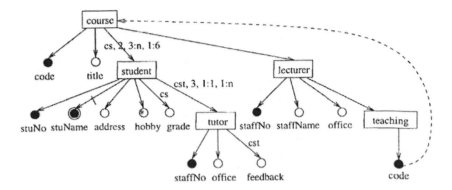

Figure 4.3. Final ORA-SS schema obtained after Step 2

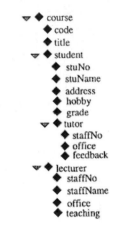

Figure 4.4. DataGuide extracted from sample XML document

4.4 Discussion

Researchers have proposed various methods to extract semistructured data schema. These include DataGuide [Goldman and Widom, 1997], and approximate graph schema [Wang et al., 2000]. Figure 4.4 shows the DataGuide that is extracted from our example XML document. We observe that the DataGuide is similar to the initial ORA-SS schema tree obtained in Step 1 of the extraction algorithm.

It is clear that DataGuide and a set of data path expressions only discover the hierarchy of the semistructured data. There is no knowledge of object classes and their identifiers, relationship types, attributes of object classes and relationship types, participation constraints, etc. These models are not able to distinguish between the different semantics of attributes such as *hobby* and *grade*. Both of these attributes are considered as subelements of the object class *student* although *grade* is a relationship attribute. Thus, the usage of these schemas is quite limited.

Compared to existing approaches which extract the structural information of XML documents, our extraction algorithm carries out additional checking and analysis of the XML document to derive semantic information.

Database designers will be aware that *stuNo* is the identifier of object class *student;* attribute *grade* belongs to a binary relationship type between *course* and *student; teaching* is an IDREFS attribute referencing to object class *course;* etc Such semantic information will lead to higher quality schemas, and facilitate all levels of database design, implementation and usage. For example, [Chen et al., 2002] gives an algorithm for designing valid XML views using ORA-SS data model; and [Mo and Ling, 2002] gives an algorithm to map ORA-SS schema to object-relational database, which can be used to store XML data efficiently. The set of tables obtained for the object-relational database is exactly the same as the final object class tables and relationship type tables (Tables 4.2 and 4.4). Details will be discussed in Chapter 7.

4.5   Summary

In this chapter, we have discussed the importance of a schema for semistructured data. We have described an algorithm to extract ORA-SS schema from XML documents. First, the algorithm generates an initial ORA-SS schema which contains structural information, and differentiates objects from attributes, and single-valued attributes from multivalued attributes. Next, the algorithm tries to infer semantic information such as whether an attribute which appears as a subelement in the XML document belongs to an object class or a relationship type, the keys of object classes, the IDREF(S) attributes, and degrees and participation constraints of relationship types, etc. User inputs are needed in this step to verify the various semantics discovered. We have demonstrated that the ability to extract a semantically rich schema from XML documents is useful and important in database design, implementation and usage.

For future work, it would be useful to extend the extraction algorithm to support additional features in the ORA-SS schema. For example, the ORA-SS schema has a concept of "ANY" attribute, which is used to capture infrequently used attributes. ORA-SS also supports ordering on instances of an object class, values of an attribute and set of attributes, and the inheritance relationship. Further, if an XML document is updated, the extract ORA-SS schema should also be modified to reflect the changes in the underlying data. It will be important to develop an efficient incremental method to maintain the extracted schema.

This page intentionally left blank

Chapter 5

NORMALIZATION

Reducing data redundancy is an important step in relational database design. Designers reduce data redundancy by normalizing the database schema to one of the normal forms (e.g. 2NF, 3NF, BCNF, 4NF etc.) using constraints on the attributes in the schema. Normalization of relational databases is recognized in the research community where it has been widely researched, and also in industry where it is regarded as a useful technique. In contrast, there has been limited research on normalization of semistructured data [Arenas and Libkin, 2004; Embley and Mok, 2001; Lee et al., 1999; Mani et al., 2001; Wu et al., 2001a].

The interest in storing semistructured data in repositories has increased with the increased use and complexity of semistructured data. Semistructured data can be stored in a native XML database, an XML enabled database, or a more traditional database such as a nested relational or relational database. Current research that maps semistructured data to a traditional database [Deutsch et al., 1999; Florescu and Kossmann, 1999; Shanmugasundaram et al., 1999] ignores the detection of redundancy, although, some of the same kinds of anomalies that arise in relational databases can arise in repositories that store semistructured data. For example, update, insertion and deletion anomalies exist in repositories that store semistructured data when information is duplicated.

In this chapter, we define a normal form for ORA-SS schema diagrams (called NF ORA-SS schema diagram) which is based on a normal form for nested relations, and describe an algorithm that maps an ORA-SS schema diagram into an NF ORA-SS schema diagram. Section 5.1 gives a example to highlight the need for normalization in semistructured data model. Section 5.2 reviews definitions from [Ling and Yan, 1994]. In Section 5.3 we define a normal form for ORA-SS schema diagrams and in Section 5.4 we describe an

78

```
<enrollment>
    <department name="CS">
        <course code="CS1102">
            <title>Data Structure</title>
            <student stuNo="stu123">
                <stuName> Zheng Zhang </stuName>
                <address>hostel 01-03-A </address>
                <grade>A</grade>
            </student>
            <student stuNo="stu125">
                <stuName> Liang Chen </stuName>
                <hobby>hockey</hobby>
                <hobby>reading</hobby>
                <grade>B</grade>
            </student>
        </course>
        <course code="CS2104">
            <student stuNo="stu123">
                <stuName> Zheng Zhang </stuName>
                <address>hostel 01-03-A</address>
            </student>
            <student stuNo="stu125">
                <stuName> Liang Chen </stuName>
                <hobby>hockey</hobby>
                <hobby>reading</hobby>
            </student>
        </course>
    </department>
</enrollment>
```

Figure 5.1. Example XML document with redundant information

algorithm that maps an ORA-SS schema diagram to an NF ORA-SS schema diagram.

5.1   Motivating Example

The following example demonstrates how redundancy can occur in semistructured data and highlights the need for normalization.

Example 5.1 *Consider the XML document in Figure 5.1 that contains information about courses in a department and the students who take the courses. In this document, there are two courses (with code CS1102 and CS2104) and two students (with stuNo stu123 and stu125). The details of the students, such as stuName, address and hobby, are repeated for each course the student takes.*

This duplication of information causes a number of problems. For example, if a student changes their address, it must be updated everywhere the address is stored, that is it must be updated in every course the student takes. If a new course is inserted and student stu125 enrolls in that course then the details of

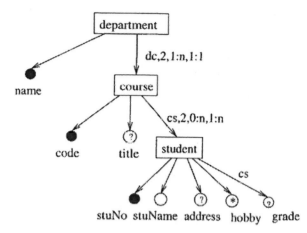

Figure 5.2. An ORA-SS schema diagram for document in Figure 5.1

this student must be entered again, correctly. If a student is enrolled in only one course and the student withdraws from the course, then the details of the student are lost. Duplication of data is likely to lead to inconsistencies when data is inserted, updated or deleted, without checking the existing data.

The ORA-SS schema diagram for the document in Figure 5.1 is shown in Figure 5.2. Recall that the root of the XML document is not copied to the ORA-SS schema diagram. Any document that is valid with respect to this schema is likely to contain redundant data which leads to the problems described above.

We would like to define a schema that represents the same constraints, but does not exhibit the same redundancy in valid documents. Such a schema is shown in Figure 5.3. A reference is created between the new object class stuRef and the object class student. The attribute of relationship type cs, grade, is connected to the object class stuRef.

Of course, an ORA-SS schema cannot be used directly by a semistructured database. Most semistructured databases support either DTD or XMLSchema. We show a DTD representation of Figure 5.3 in Figure 5.4. The data in the XML document in Figure 5.1 must be transformed to match the structure of the schema in Figure 5.4. The transformed XML document is shown in Figure 5.5. In the transformed XML document the information about students, namely stuName, address and hobby, are stored only once.

As noted previously the detection of redundant data has been researched in other data models, and algorithms have been described to design schemas that eliminate the redundant data. The most well understood research is in the area of relational databases, where a series of database normal forms such as 3NF, 4NF and 5NF, have been proposed to determine whether a set of relations

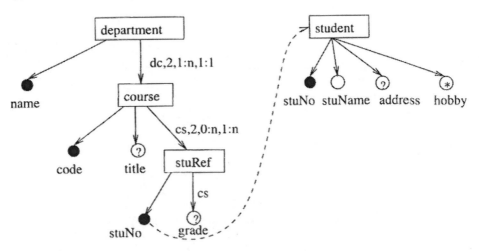

Figure 5.3. An ORA-SS schema diagram, where valid documents do not contain redundant information

```
<!ELEMENT enrollment  (department+, student+)>
<!ELEMENT department   (course+)>
    <!ATTLIST department  name  ID  #REQUIRED>
<!ELEMENT  course  (title?, stuRef*)>
    <!ATTLIST course  code  ID  #REQUIRED>
<!ELEMENT title  (#PCDATA)>
<!ELEMENT student  (stuName, address?, hobby*)>
    <!ATTLIST student stuNo ID #REQUIRED>
<!ELEMENT stuName  (#PCDATA)>
<!ELEMENT address (#PCDATA)>
<!ELEMENT hobby (#PCDATA)>
<!ELEMENT stuRef  (grade?))>
    <!ATTLIST stuRef  stuNo IDREF #REQUIRED>
<!ELEMENT grade  (#PCDATA)>
```

Figure 5.4. A DTD for the schema diagram in Figure 5.3

is a good design for a given database. A common way to design relational databases is to model the requirements using ER diagrams. In order to combine requirements modeling and normalization, [Ling, 1985] proposed a normal form for ER diagrams, which ensured that all the relations mapped from ER diagrams are in a normal form, such as in 3NF or 5NF.

The concept of normalization has been extended to the nested relational data model, where normal forms such as NNF (Nested Normal Form) [Ozsoyoglu and Yuan, 1987] and NF-NR (Normal Form for Nested Relation) [Ling and Yan, 1994] have been proposed to guarantee good properties for the underlying nested relational databases.

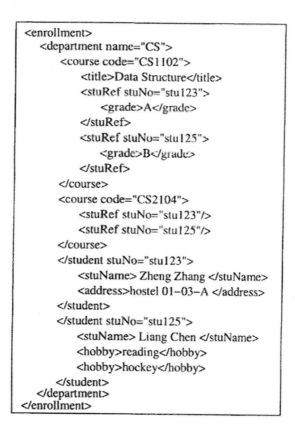

```
<enrollment>
    <department name="CS">
        <course code="CS1102">
            <title>Data Structure</title>
            <stuRef stuNo="stu123">
                <grade>A</grade>
            </stuRef>
            <stuRef stuNo="stu125">
                <grade>B</grade>
            </stuRef>
        </course>
        <course code="CS2104">
            <stuRef stuNo="stu123"/>
            <stuRef stuNo="stu125"/>
        </course>
        </student stuNo="stu123">
            <stuName> Zheng Zhang </stuName>
            <address>hostel 01-03-A </address>
        </student>
        </student stuNo="stu125">
            <stuName> Liang Chen </stuName>
            <hobby>reading</hobby>
            <hobby>hockey</hobby>
        </student>
    </department>
</enrollment>
```

Figure 5.5. Example XML document without redundant information

We observe that the ORA-SS data model is similar to the nested relational data model in that they both have a tree-like structure and allow nested relations or multiple occurrences of objects. Hence, starting from the root of a given ORA-SS schema diagram D, we can easily construct a nested relation R, which has the single valued attributes of D's root object class as its atomic attributes, and the multivalued attributes and composite attributes as well as the child object classes (including all its child object classes that have disjunctive relationships) of D's root object class as its nested relations. For example, the nested relation for the ORA-SS schema diagram in Figure 5.2 is

department(
  name, course (
    code, title, student (
      stuNo, stuName, address, hobby*, grade)*)*)

The root object class *department* is the name of the nested relation. The single valued attribute *name* is an attribute of relation department. The object class *course* becomes a level 1 nested relation, nested within *department*, with attributes *code* and *title*. The object class *student* is a level 2 nested relation, nested within course. The nested relation *student* has attributes *stuNo, stuName, address, grade,* and a nested relation *hobby(hobby)** which we express in its short form, *hobby**. The "*" indicates that the relation is repeating, for example a student has many hobbies, a course has many students, and a department has many courses. We can construct a set of nested relations for an ORA-SS schema diagram that consists of several separated tree-structured components (each starting from different roots and perhaps related to others through reference semantics). As an illustration, the corresponding nested relations for the ORA-SS schema diagram in Figure 5.3 is

> *department (name, course (code, title, stuRef (stuNo, grade)*)*)*
> *student (stuNo, stuName, address, hobby*)*

While the tree structured data models, including ORA-SS, nested relations and OEM, can represent hierarchical data (or 1-to-many relationships) in a direct and natural way, they have problems representing many-to-many relationships. In particular, duplication of data occurs when many-to-many relationships or relationships involving more than two participating object classes are represented.

The update anomalies in XML documents and the hierarchical representation of the data in XML documents motivates the need for defining a normal form ORA-SS schema diagram. The correspondences between the ORA-SS data model and the nested relational data model suggest that we can say an ORA-SS schema diagram is in a normal form if its corresponding set of nested relations is in *normal form for the set of nested relations* (NF-NR), as defined in [Ling, 1989; Ling and Yan, 1994]. The goal is that XML documents that conform to a DTD or XML Schema generated from a normal form ORA-SS schema diagram have no redundancy and no undesirable update anomalies.

5.2   Background

The definition for a normal form ORA-SS schema diagram is based on the definition of NF-NR for nested relations, which is described in [Ling and Yan, 1994]. We start by introducing definitions that are needed in the following sections. The definition of NF-NR for nested relations is based on the concepts of extended functional dependency (EFD) and the level of a relation.

An extended functional dependency (EFD) is like a functional dependency except that it can also describe a constraint between a single-valued attribute and a nested relation.

For example, the extended functional dependency

$$stuNo \Rightarrow hobby$$

represents the constraint, whenever two tuples agree on the value of all attributes in *stuNo,* they also agree on the value of all attributes in *hobby.* An extended functional dependency that involves only single valued attributes maps to a functional dependency.
   For example,

$stuNo \Rightarrow address$ **can be mapped to** $stuNo \rightarrow address$

An extended functional dependency where a single valued attribute determines a nested relation maps to a multivalued dependency, so the extended functional dependency

$stuNo \Rightarrow hobby$ **can be mapped to** $stuNo \twoheadrightarrow hobby$

We extend the term transitively dependent to apply to nested relations. If there is a relation $R(a, b, c(d)^*)$ and $a \rightarrow b$ and $b \Rightarrow c$, then we say that c is transitively dependent on a.
   The definition of NF-NR also refers to the concept of a level of a nested relation in a nested relation. The **level** of a nested relation that is not nested within another relation is zero. The level of a nested relation is 1 greater than the level of the relation it is nested within.

Example 5.2 *Consider the nested relation*

> *department(*
>   *name, course (*
>   *code, title, student (*
>   *stuNo, stuName, address, grade, hobby*)*)*)*

From the definition above, we have:

> $level(department) = 0,$
> $level(course) = 1,$
> $level(student) = 2,$
> $level(hobby) = 3.$

   We are now able to introduce the definition for normal form for nested relations (NF-NR) which we use in the following section when defining NF ORA-SS schema diagrams. In the following NF-NR definition, we use the notation

K_R to denote the key of relation R, and $ATTR(R)$ to denote the attributes of R.

Definition 5.1 A *nested relation R with level(R) = 0 is in* **normal form for nested relation (NF-NR)** *iff:*

1 *R has at least one key.*

2 *All the single valued attributes of R form a 3NF relation with all keys of R as its keys.*

3 *If there is no nested relation in R and all the attributes of R form the key of R, then R is also in 4NF.*

4 *For each nested relation R_1 of R, and any key K of R, the fallowing holds:*

   (a) *there exists no A, $A \subset ATTR(R_1)$, such that $K \twoheadrightarrow A$.*

   (b) *R_1 is not transitively dependent on K.*

5 *For each nested relation R_1 of R, all the attributes of R_1 and K_R form a nested relation in NF-NR.*

6 *For any nested relation R_1 of R, $K_R \cap K_{R_1} = \emptyset$ or $K_R \subset K_{R_1}$.*

The intuition of the definition for NF-NR for nested relations depends on a number of conditions. A nested relation is in NF-NR if its single valued attributes are in 3NF and 4NF. None of the attributes of the nested relations have a multivalued or transitive dependency on the key of the relation. A nested relation formed from the attributes of a nested relation and the key of the ancestor relations must be in NF-NR. Finally either the key of the relation and key of the nested relation are disjoint, or the key of the relation must be a subset of the key of the nested relation.

Example 5.3 *In this example, we examine two nested relations. Let us first consider the following employee nested relation and the associated functional dependencies:*

$$emp(\ emp\#,\ name,\ address,\ child*,\ sal\_history(date,\ salary)*)$$
$$emp\# \rightarrow name, address$$
$$emp\# \Rightarrow child, sal\_history(date, salary)$$
$$emp\#, date \rightarrow salary$$

We consider each of the conditions in the definition of NF-NR in turn.

1 *The nested relation emp has at least one key, emp#.*

2 *The relation emp(emp#, name, address) is in 3NF.*

3 *There are nested relations in emp.*

4 *We first consider the nested relation child. There are no attributes in child that are multivalue determined by the emp#, and child is not transitively dependent on emp#. We next consider the nested relation sal_history. There are no attributes in sal_history that are multivalue determined by the emp#, and sal_history is not transitively dependent on emp#.*

5 *We again consider both the nested relations child and sal_history respec tively. The relations (emp#, child) and (emp#, date, salary) are both in NF-NR.*

6 *Finally emp# ⊂ {emp#, child} and emp# ⊂ {emp#, date}.*

Each of the conditions are satisfied so nested relation emp is in NF-NR.

Next, let us consider the following department nested relation:

> *department(*
> > *name, course (*
> > > *code, title, student (*
> > > > *stuNo, stuName, address, grade)*)*)*

Since a course is taught in only one department, there is an extended functional dependency, name ⇒ course. However, each student has a unique student number, so stuNo → stuName. From condition 5 of the NF-NR definition, the nested relation department is not in NF-NR if the nested relation formed from the key of course and the attributes of student are not in NF-NR. The nested relation (name, code, stuNo, stuName, address, grade) is not in 3NF since stuNo → stuName.

The nested relation department is not in NF-NR.

5.3   A Normal Form For Semistructured Schemas

The concept of a normal form (NF) ORA-SS schema diagram depends on the twin concepts of an object class normal form (O-NF) and a relationship type normal form (R-NF). The structure of the definition is in the style of [Ling, 1985], where the authors define entity and relationship normal forms for an Entity-Relationship diagram. The definitions of O-NF and R-NF both depend on the definition of NF-NR, which is described in the previous section.

Definition 5.2 *An object class O of an ORA-SS schema diagram is said to be in* **object class normal form** *(O-NF), if a nested relation constructed from*

- *O's single-valued simple attributes as its atomic attributes,*

- *O's dependent object classes, multivalued attributes and composite attributes as its nested relations,*

is in normal form NF-NR.

Definition 5.3 *A relationship type R of an ORA-SS schema diagram D is said to be in* **relationship type normal form** *(R-NF), if a nested relation constructed from*

- *the identifiers of the participating object classes as its single values atomic attributes,*

- *R's single valued simple attributes as its atomic attributes, and*

- *R's multivalued and composite attributes as its repeating groups,*

is in normal form NF-NR.

We now consider examples that violate the O-NF and R-NF conditions. In each example, we provide a schema where the conditions are violated and a corresponding schema where the conditions are not violated but we do not describe the transformation from the original schema to the new schema until Section 5.4.

Example 5.4 *Consider the lecturer object class given in Figure 5.6(a). Assume we have the following functional dependencies:*

$$staffNo \rightarrow sName, dept,$$
$$dept \rightarrow faculty.$$

The nested relation constructed from this object class is

lecturer (staffNo, sName, dept, faculty).

The relation constructed from the single valued attributes of the nested relation lecturer is not in 3NF, since staffNo $\rightarrow$ faculty is a transitive dependency, and as a consequence the nested relation lecturer is not in NF-NR. Hence the condition in the O-NF definition is violated, and object class lecturer is not in O-NF. Both object classes, lecturer and department, in Figure 5.6(b) are in O-NF.

Example 5.5 *Consider the ORA-SS schema diagram in Figure 5.7(a). The schema represents the constraints that the lecturer can teach any of the courses using the textbooks as prescribed for the course, and is designed as a ternary*

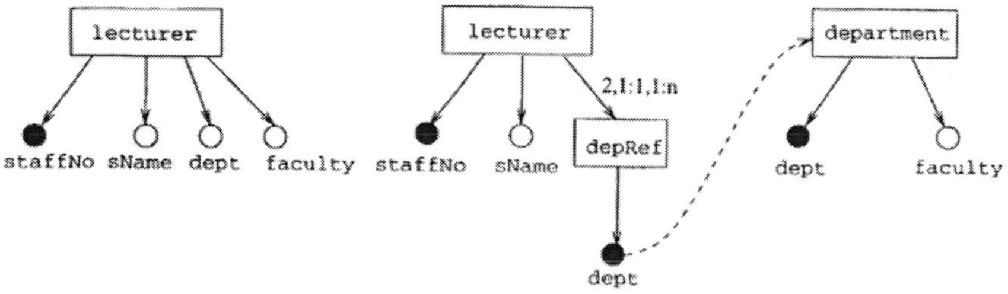

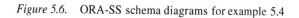

(a) Object class *lecturer* is not in O–NF since *faculty* is transitively dependent on *staffNo* via *dept*

(b) Object classes *lecturer* and *department* are in O–NF

Figure 5.6. ORA-SS schema diagrams for example 5.4

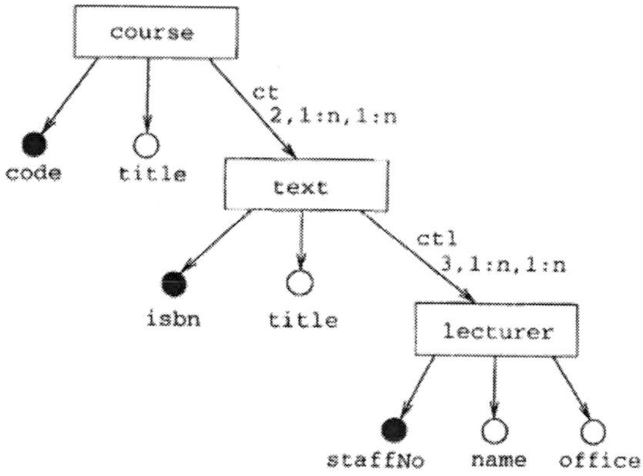

(a) Relationship type *ctl* is not in R–NF since *code* ->> *isbn*|*staffNo*

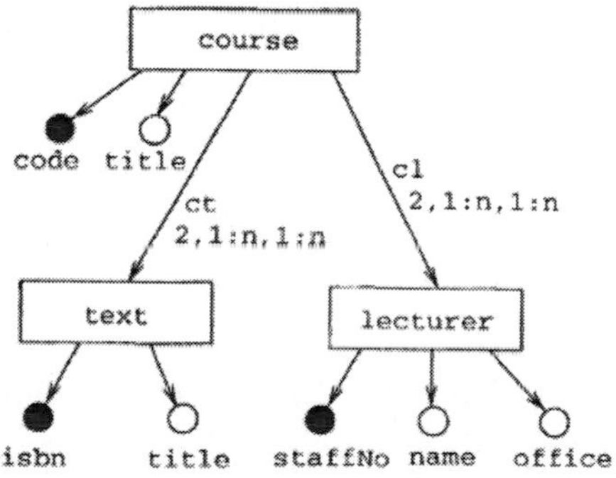

(b) Both relationship types *ct* and *cl* are in R–NF

Figure 5.7. ORA-SS schema diagrams for example 5.5

relationship among course, text and lecturer. The textbooks of a course should be independent of the lecturer that teaches the course, i.e., the following multivalued dependency (MVD) exists:

$$code \twoheadrightarrow isbn \mid staffNo.$$

Consider the nested relation ctl (code, isbn, staffNo) built from the identifiers of the participating object classes and attributes of the relationship type ctl. This nested relation is not in NF-NR since the corresponding relation is not in 4NF because of the above MVD. The condition in the R-NF definition is violated, and therefore the relationship type ctl is not in R-NF. A schema diagram in which both relationship types, ct and cl, are in R-NF is shown in Figure 5.7(b). The object class lecturer is promoted to be a direct child of the object class course.

We are now in a position to define a normal form for ORA-SS schema diagrams.

Definition 5.4 *An ORA-SS schema diagram D is in **normal form** (NF) if and only if it satisfies the following five conditions:*

1 *Every object class O in D is in O-NF.*

2 *Every relationship type R in D is in R-NF.*

3 *The following two cases are satisfied:*

    (a) *If R is a binary relationship type with parent object class A and child object class B, and either B is a dependent object class that has an IDD relationship type with A, or R is a one-to-many or one-to-one relationship type from A to B then all B's attributes are connected to B, and all the attributes of R are connected to B.*

    (b) *If R is an n-ary relationship type with n (n>2) participating object classes $O_1, O_2, \ldots, O_n$, and the path going from the top of D linking those object classes is $/O_1/O_2/ \ldots /O_n$ then for each object class O_i ($2 \leq i \leq n$)*

        (i) *O_i has an i-ary relationship type R_i with ancestor object classes $O_1, O_2, \ldots, O_{i-1}$.*

        (ii) *If O_i is a dependent object class that has an IDD relationship type with its ancestors, or the functional dependency between O_i and its ancestors, $O_i \rightarrow O_1, O_2, \ldots, O_{i-1}$, can be derived from the dependency constraints specified for the schema then the attributes of O_i are connected to object class O_i, and the attributes of R_i are connected to O_i.*

4 *There is no relationship type nested under another many-to-many or many-to-one binary or n-ary (n>2) relationship type.*

5 *No attribute or relationship type can be derived from other attributes and/or relationship types in D.*

Recall that the goal of defining a normal form for ORA-SS schema diagrams is to reduce the anomalies in instances of the schema. How does the definition of NF ORA-SS schema diagrams achieve this? Condition 1 ensures there are no redundancies within object classes, while condition 2 ensures there are no redundancies within relationship types. Condition 3(a) and 3(b)ii ensure that the attributes of object classes and relationship types are connected to the correct object class for binary and n-ary (where $n > 2$) relationship types respectively without storing redundant data. Condition 3(b)i ensures that the relationship types are connected to the correct object class for n-ary (where $n > 2$) relationship types. Condition 4 deals with relationship types that are not well suited to tree structured data models, namely many-to-one and many-to-many relationship types. If these relationship types have nested relationship types then there will be redundancy, so condition 4 ensures this type of nesting does not occur. Condition 5 removes global redundancies among a set of components in an ORA-SS schema diagram.

Other normal forms proposed for semistructured data, such as S3-NF [Lee et al., 1999] and XNF [Embley and Mok, 2001] deal only with the simpler functional dependencies, as we will show in Section 5.5.

Example 5.6 *Consider the ORA-SS schema diagram in Figure 5.8. If examined individually, the object classes lecturer and employee are both in O-NF, and the relationship types are in R-NF. However, if a lecturer is also an employee (i.e. lecturer(staffNo) $\subseteq$ employee(staffNo)), then some information about lecturer can also be derived from the details of employees as shown in Figure 5.8(b). The schema for the database is not in normal form since the staffNo, staffName and qualification of lecturer can be derived from that of employee, which violates condition 5 in Definition 5.4. As a consequence, staffNo, staffName and qual information for a lecturer will be repeated in instances of this schema. Figure 5.9 shows an NF ORA-SS schema diagram with a reference between lecturer and employee.*

In this section, we have defined normal form ORA-SS schema diagrams. In the next section, Section 5.4, we describe an algorithm for transforming an ORA-SS schema diagram into an NF ORA-SS schema diagram.

5.4   Converting Schemas into the Normal Form

We introduce two approaches for designing semistructured databases using ORA-SS schema diagrams. The first approach is based on the users' require-

90

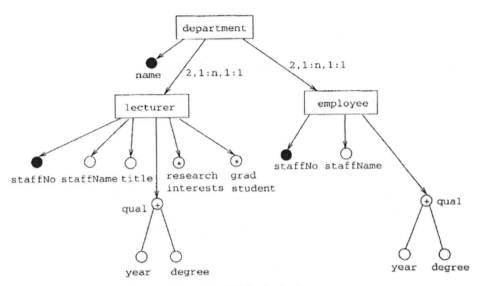

(a) An ORA–SS schema diagram with global redundancies

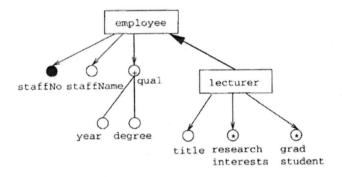

(b) ORA–SS inheritance diagram for object classes in (a)

Figure 5.8. ORA-SS schema diagram that is not in NF

ments, which are initially represented in an ORA-SS schema diagram. We convert the schema diagram into an NF ORA-SS schema diagram, and we map the normalized schema to a DTD or XML Schema. The second approach is, given a semistructured data instance, like an XML document, we can design a schema as follows:

1 Extract the schema from the XML documents using the schema extracting techniques outlined in Chapter 4.

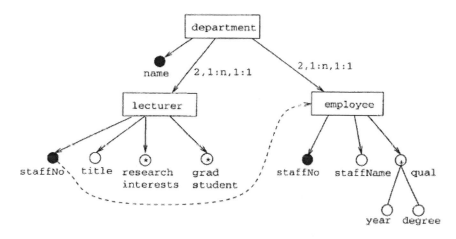

Figure 5.9. An NF ORA-SS schema diagram for Figure 5.8

2 Convert the ORA-SS schema diagram into an NF ORA-SS schema diagram.

3 Map the NF ORA-SS schema diagram to a DTD or XML Schema.

4 Restructure the initial XML documents to conform to the generated DTD or XML Schema.

A key step in the above two approaches is to convert an ORA-SS schema diagram to an NF ORA-SS schema diagram. The following conversion algorithm takes as input an ORA-SS schema diagram and the dependency constraints specified on the schema, and returns an NF ORA-SS schema diagram. The design steps provide a procedure for deriving NF ORA-SS schema diagrams.

The first step of the algorithm transforms non O-NF object classes to object classes that are in O-NF, and normally follows one of the two common approaches. In one approach a new object class is created and it becomes a child of the original object class. This approach is followed where there is a transitive dependency among the attributes of the original object class. The other approach is achieved by creating a new object class which references the original object class.

The second step in the algorithm involves transforming non R-NF relationship types into relationship types that are in R NF. This is typically achieved by moving existing object classes to more appropriate positions in the ORA-SS schema diagram. This transformation is illustrated in Example 5.5. The transformations are similar to those for nested relations, which can be found in

[Ling and Yan, 1994].

Algorithm ConvertNF

Input: an ORA-SS schema diagram *SD*, and a set of specified dependency constraints.
Output: an NF ORA-SS schema diagram.

Step 1: Convert each object class O in *SD* into O-NF.

Step 2: Convert each relationship type R in *SD* into R-NF.

Step 3: Construct separate ORA-SS schema diagrams for each object class in *SD* with its attributes.

Step 4: For each binary relationship type R from object class O_A to O_B in *SD*, assume R is described by a relationship type label L, *name* $(O_A, O_B), 2, p, c$.

> If R is an IDD relationship type (i.e., O_B is a dependent object class), or a one-to-many ($O_B \rightarrow O_A$) or one-to-one relationship type,
> **then** nest O_B along with its attributes under O_A, and tag the edge between them with L. Attach all the attributes of R to O_B, and tag the edges between attributes and O_B with the name of R
> **else** (R is not an IDD relationship type, and R is either a many-to-one ($O_A \rightarrow O_B$) or a many-to-many relationship type), construct a reference object class O'_B referencing O_B, and nest O'_B under O_A. Tag the edge between O_A and O'_B with L. Attach all the attributes of R to O'_B, and tag the edges between attributes and O'_B with the name of R.

Step 5: For each n-ary relationship type R $(n > 2)$ with participating object classes $O_1, O_2, \ldots, O_n$ in *SD*, assume the path that links those object classes is $/O_1/O_2/ \ldots /O_n$. Let R_i $(2 \leq i \leq n)$ represent the relationship from O_{i-1} to O_i, then R can be represented by a sequence of relationships $< R_2, \ldots, R_n >$. Assume each R_i is described by a relationship type label L_i, *name* $(O_1, \ldots, O_i), i, p, c$.

> **If** either O_i is a dependent object class or $O_i \rightarrow O_1, O_2, \ldots, O_{i-1}$ can be derived from the specified dependency constraints for *SD*,

then nest O_i along with its attributes under O_{i-1}, and tag the edge between them with L_i. Attach all the attributes of R_i to O_i, and tag the edges between attributes and O_i with the name of R_i, **else** (O_i is not a dependent object class, or $O_i \not\to O_1, O_2, \ldots, O_{i-1}$), construct a reference object class O'_i referencing O_i, and nest O'_i under O_{i-1}. Tag the edge between R_{i-1} and O'_i with L_i. Attach all the attributes of R_i to O'_i, and tag the edges between attributes and O'_i with the name of R_i.

Step 6: Remove redundant relationship types and redundant attributes from object classes. If a relationship type R is redundant, then the information provided by R can be derived from other relationship types, such that data will be redundant in the underlying instance. To detect a redundant relationship type, we require more information about the semantic meaning of the relationship types, which can be provided by the database designer. Some information about redundant attributes is available from the ORA-SS inheritance diagram.

We have not considered the case where there is a binary relationship type between object classes O_A, and O_C, and they are separated by one or more other object classes, or where there is an n-ary relationship type (n>2) and the participating object classes are separated by one or more object classes that don't participate in the relationship type. We leave these cases as an exercise for the reader.

We can prove informally that any ORA-SS schema diagram generated using Algorithm ConvertNF is an NF ORA-SS schema diagram. Step 1 in Algorithm ConvertNF ensures that every object class is in O-NF, satisfying condition 1 in Definition 5.4. Step 2 ensures that every relationship type is in R-NF satisfying condition 2 in Definition 5.4.

Steps 3, 4 and 5 deal with relationship types.

In step 4, binary relationship types, where the relationship type is either an IDD relationship type or a one-to-many or one-to-one relationship type, are reintroduced with attributes connected to either the object class to which they belong or the relationship type to which they belong. This part of step 4 satisfies condition 3(a) in Definition 5.4.

In step 5, n-ary relationship types (n>2), where the relationship type is either an IDD relationship type or the child object class functionally determines the other object classes involved in the relationship are reintroduced with attributes connected to either the object class to which they belong or the relationship type to which they belong. This part of step 5 satisfies condition 3(b) in Definition 5.4.

94

In step 4, binary relationship types, where the relationship type is a many-to-one or many-to-many relationship type are addressed by creating a new object class and including a reference between the original child object class and the new object class. The attributes are connected to either the object class or relationship type to which they belong.

In step 5, n-ary relationship types (n>2), where the child object class is not a dependent object class and the child object class does not functionally determine the other object classes involved in the relationship type are addressed by creating a new object class and introducing a reference between the original child object class and the new object class. These parts of steps 4 and 5 satisfy condition 4 in Definition 5.4.

Step 6 deals with redundant relationship types and redundant object classes, and satisfies condition 5 of Definition 5.4.

Hence all conditions in Definition 5.4 are satisfied, so any ORA-SS schema diagram generated using Algorithm ConvertNF is an NF ORA-SS schema diagram.

We illustrate Algorithm ConvertNF in the following five examples. Example 5.7 illustrates how many-to-many relationship types are dealt with in the algorithm. Example 5.8 demonstrates a ternary relationship type. Example 5.9 demonstrates how the algorithm deals with object classes that are not already in O-NF, while Example 5.10 contains an IDD relationship type, and Example 5.11 contains attributes that can be derived from other attributes.

Example 5.7 *Consider the ORA-SS schema diagram in Figure 5.10(a). There is a many-to-many binary relationship type lc between lecturer and course, and a many-to-many binary relationship type ct between course and textbook. There is an attribute feedback that belongs to relationship type lc.*

Step 1: *We consider each object class individually. The nested relations formed for the object class lecturer, course, and textbook are*

$$lecturer(\underline{staffNo}, name),$$
$$course(\underline{code}, title),$$
$$textbook(\underline{ISBN}, author^*, title)$$

Each nested relation is in NF-NR so each object class lecturer, course and textbook is in O-NF.

Step 2: *We consider each relationship type individually. The nested relations formed for the relationship types lc and ct are*

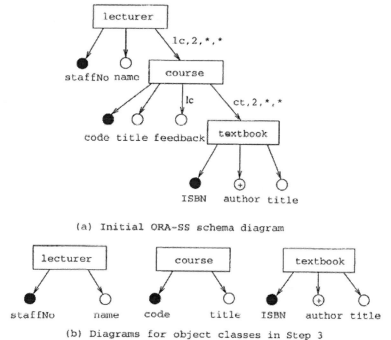

(a) Initial ORA-SS schema diagram

(b) Diagrams for object classes in Step 3

Figure 5.10. Figures for Example 5.7 illustrating Algorithm ConvertNF

$$lc(\underline{staffNo}, \underline{code}, feedback),$$
$$ct(\underline{code}, \underline{ISBN}),$$

Each nested relation is in NF-NR so each relationship type lc and ct is in R-NF.

Step 3: *We generate three schema diagrams for the object classes with attributes as shown in Figure 5.10(b).*

Step 4: *We represent the binary relationship type lc. Since lc is a many-to-many relationship type from lecturer to course, we create a reference object class courseRef referencing course and nest courseRef under lecturer, as shown in Figure 5.11(a). The attribute feedback is attached to courseRef, and the edge between courseRef and feedback is tagged with lc.*
Then, we represent the binary relationship type ct. Since ct is a many-to-many relationship type from course to textbook, we create a reference object class textbookRef referencing textbook and nest textbookRef under course, as shown in Figure 5.11(b).

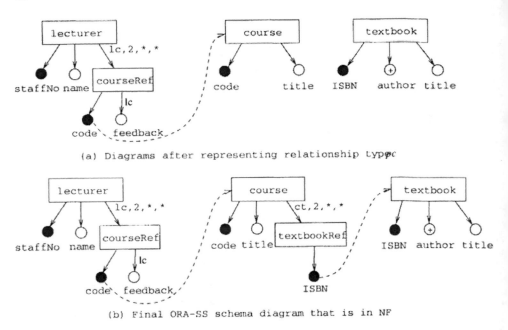

(a) Diagrams after representing relationship type c

(b) Final ORA-SS schema diagram that is in NF

Figure 5.11. Figures for Example 5.7 illustrating Algorithm ConvertNF

Step 5: *There are no n-ary (n > 2) relationship types.*

Step 6: *There are no redundant relationship types or attributes.*

The schema diagram in Figure 5.11(b) is in normal form.

The above example illustrates the normalization process by removing redundancy caused by many-to-many relationship types. The process to remove redundancy due to n-ary relationship types is illustrated in the following example.

Example 5.8 *From the ORA-SS schema diagram D in Figure 5.12(a) we can derive the following functional dependencies. Because of the child participation constraint 1 : 1 in the label of the ternary relationship cst*

$$course, student \rightarrow tutor.$$

Since code, stuNo and staffNo are the identifiers of course, student and tutor respectively,

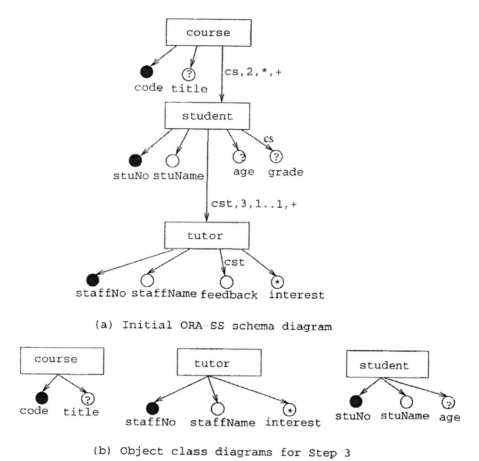

Figure 5.12. Figures for Example 5.8 illustrating Algorithm ConvertNF

$$code, stuNo \rightarrow staffNo.$$

There is a binary relationship type cs between course and student and a ternary relationship type cst among course, student and tutor. Grade is an attribute of the binary relationship cs, and feedback is an attribute of the ternary relationship cst.

Step 1: *We consider each object class individually. The nested relations formed for the object classes course, student, and tutor are*

$course(\underline{code}, title),$
$student(\underline{stuNo}, stuName, age),$

$$tutor(\underline{staffNo}, staffName, interest^*)$$

Each nested relation is in NF-NR so each object class course, student and tutor is in O-NF.

Step 2: *We consider each relationship type individually. The nested relations formed for the relationship types cs and cst are*

$$cs(\underline{code, stuNo}, grade),$$
$$cst(\underline{code, stuNo}, staffNo, feedback),$$

Since the child participation constraint of relationship type cst is 1 : 1, *the identifier of the nested relation cst is code, stuNo (rather than the expected code, stuNo, staffNo). Each nested relation is in NF-NR so each relationship type lc and cr is in R-NF.*

Step 3: *We generate three schema diagrams for the object classes course, student and tutor, as shown in Figure 5.12(b).*

Step 4: *We represent the binary relationship type cs as shown in Figure 5.13(a). Since cs is a many-to-many relationship type from course to student, we create a reference object class stuRef referencing student and nest stuRef under course. Relationship attribute grade is connected to stuRef.*

Step 5: *The ternary relationship cst is considered. Since*

tutor → student, course

cannot be derived from the given functional dependency constraints, we create a reference object class tutorRef referencing tutor, and nest tutorRef under stuRef as shown in Figure 5.13(b). Relationship attribute feedback is connected to tutorRef.

Step 6: *There are no redundant attributes or relationship types.*

The diagram shown in Figure 5.13(b) is now in normal form.

In the above two examples, the object classes of the given schema are initially in object normal form (O-NF). We now illustrate the normalization process when the given object classes are not in O-NF.

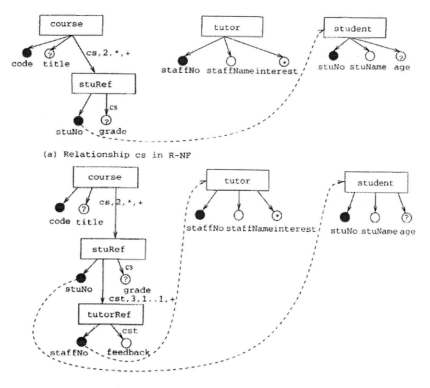

(a) Relationship cs in R-NF

(b)ORA-SS schema diagram that is in NF

Figure 5.13. Figures for Example 5.8 illustrating Algorithm ConvertNF

Example 5.9 *Consider the object class student given in Figure 5.14(a). We have the following functional dependency:*

uniName → country.

From the diagram, we have:

stuNo → uni(uniName, country), stuName, address   so

stuNo → uniName, country, stuName, address

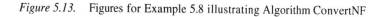

Step 1: *Consider the nested relation formed from the attributes of object class student,*

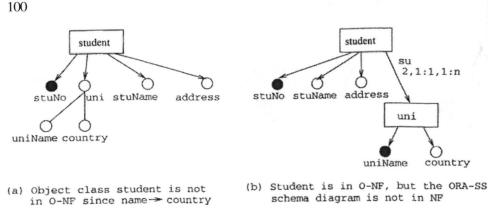

(a) Object class student is not
in O-NF since name → country

(b) Student is in O-NF, but the ORA-SS
schema diagram is not in NF

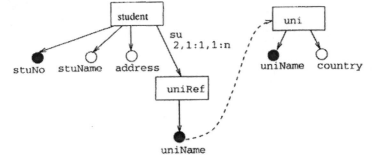

(c) Normalized ORA-SS schema diagram

Figure 5.14. Figures for Example 5.9 illustrating Algorithm ConvertNF

student (*stuNo*, uni (uniName, country), stuName, address).

where uni is a composite single valued attribute of the student relation. This
nested relation is not in NF-NR, since country is transitively dependent on
stuNo. Following Algorithm ConvertNF, we create a new object class named
uni with uniName and country as its identifier and attribute respectively, then
we generate a many-to-one relationship type su from student to uni.

Step 2: *Relationship type su is in R-NF.*

Step 3: *Separate schema diagrams are created for object classes student
and uni.*

Step 4: *We observe that relationship type su is a many-to-one relationship
type, so the schema diagram obtained in Figure 5.14 (b) is still not an NF ORA-
SS schema diagram. A new object class uniRef is created and a reference is*

introduced between uniRef and uni.

Steps 5 and 6: *There are no n-ary relationships in the ORA-SS diagram, and no redundant attributes or relationship types.*

The final result shown in Figure 5.14(c) is now in normal form.

Next, we illustrate the process of transforming an ORA-SS schema with an IDD relationship type into its normal form.

Example 5.10 *Consider the ORA-SS schema diagram in Figure 5.15(a), with an IDD binary relationship type from employee to dependent. We have the following functional dependency:*

$$school \rightarrow schoolAddress$$

Step 1: *Consider the nested relation formed from the attributes of object class employee,*

employee (staffNo, dependent (depName, school, schoolAddress, hobby*)).

This nested relation is not in NF-NR, since schoolAddress is transitively dependent on {staffNo, depName}. Following Algorithm ConvertNF, we create a new object class named school with school and schoolAddress as its identifier and attribute respectively, then we generate a many-to-one relationship type ds from dependent to school, as shown in Figure 5.15(b).

Step 2: *Relationship type ds is in R-NF.*

Step 3: *Separate schema diagrams are created for object classes employee and school.*

Step 4: *We observe that relationship type ds is a many-to-one relationship type, so the schema diagram obtained in Figure 5.15 (b) is still not an NF ORA-SS schema diagram. A new object class schoolRef is created and a reference is introduced between schoolRef and school.*

Steps 5 and 6: *There are no n-ary relationships in the ORA-SS diagram, and no redundant attributes or relationship types.*

The final example illustrates normalization of an ORA-SS diagram with redundant attributes.

102

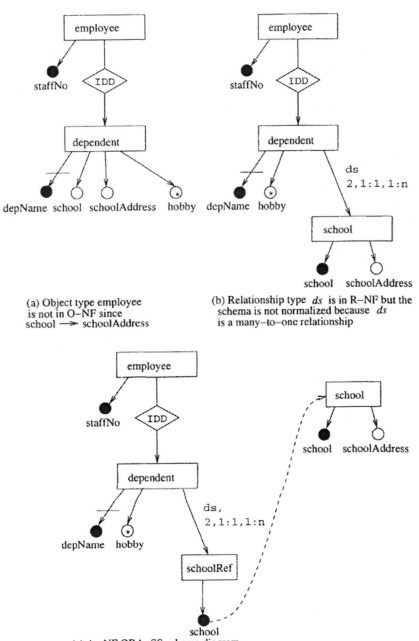

(a) Object type employee
is not in O–NF since
school ⟶ schoolAddress

(b) Relationship type *ds* is in R–NF but the
schema is not normalized because *ds*
is a many–to–one relationship

(c) An NF ORA–SS schema diagram

Figure 5.15.   Figures for Example 5.10 illustrating Algorithm ConvertNF

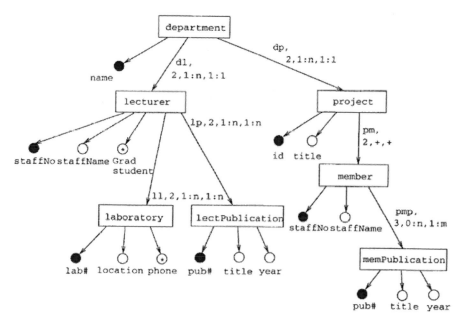

Figure 5.16. Figures for Example 5.11 illustrating Algorithm ConvertNF

Example 5.11 *Consider the ORA-SS schema diagram in Figure 5.16. Each department has a name, information about the lecturers working in the department and information about the research projects undertaken within the department. The lecturer information consists of staffNo, staffName, grad students, and information about the laboratories he/she works in as well as his/her publications; the project information consists of an id, the participating members (lecturers), and members publications on that project.*

Step 1: *The nested relations formed for each of the object classes are in NF-NR so the corresponding object classes are in O-NF.*

Step 2: *The nested relations formed for each of the relationship types are in NF-NR so the corresponding relationship types are in R-NF.*

Step 3: *We generate seven schema diagrams for the object classes.*

Step 4: *We recognize that the binary relationship types ll, lp and pm are many-to-many relationship types. A new object class is created for each of the children object classes in these relationship types, and a reference is intro-*

104

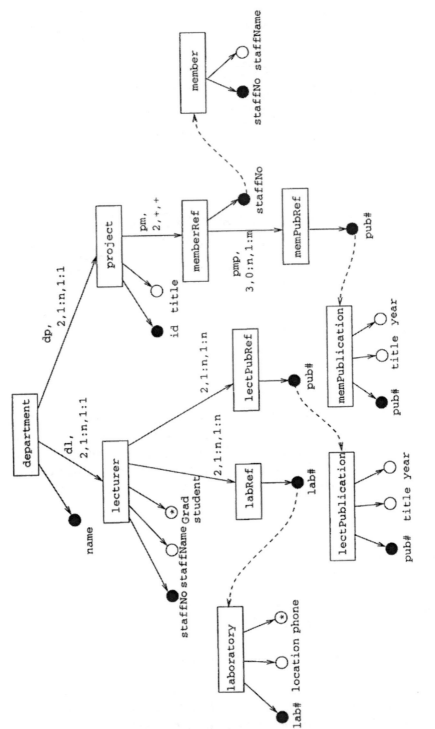

Figure 5.17. Figures for Example 5.11 illustrating Algorithm ConvertNF

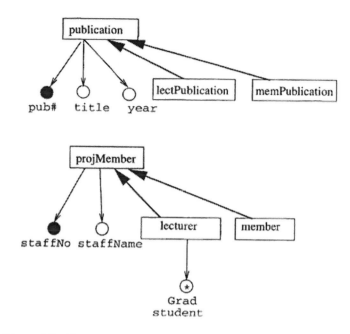

Figure 5.18. Figures for Example 5.11 illustrating Algorithm ConvertNF

duced between the new object class and the original.

Step 5: *We recognize that in the ternary relationship type pmp (in Figure 5.16)*

$$memPublication \nrightarrow member, project, department,$$

so we generate an object class memPubRef under memberRef, and let the object class memPubRef reference memPublication as shown in Figure 5.17.

Step 6: *The members of projects are lecturers and research assistants, so the details of lecturers will not only be stored in a relationship with department objects but also in a relationship with project objects. In order to remove this replication a new object class is created which is referenced by both member and lecturer. However, because the new object class has the same attributes as the object class member (as shown in the inheritance diagram in Figure 5.18), we are able to replace the new object class with a reference object class member.*

Because some of the lecturers are members of projects, some publications that are instances of memPublication are also instances of lectPublication.

106

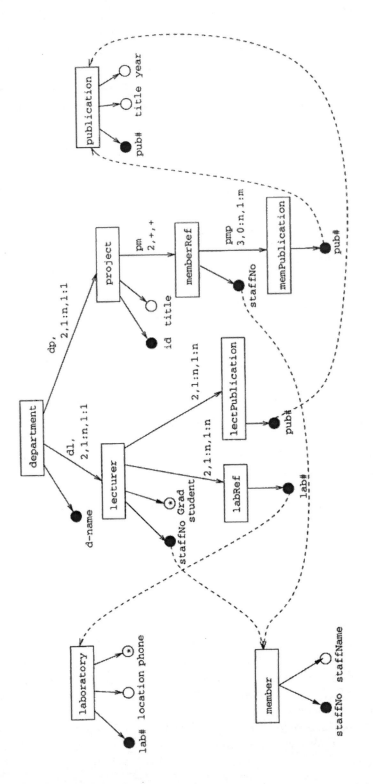

Figure 5.19. Figures for Example 5.11 illustrating Algorithm ConvertNF

In order to remove this replication a new object class is created which is refer-
enced by both memPublication and lectPublication. Because the object class
publication has the same attributes as both object classes lectPublication
and memPublication (as shown in Figure 5.18), we are able to remove both
object classes. If all the publications of lecturers were published by members
of a project, then we could remove lectPublication. However, since some lec-
turers may not work on projects or may have publications other than those that
are published as part of a project, we retain lectPublication.

The ORA-SS schema diagram shown in Figure 5.19 is now in normal form.

5.5   Discussion

In a survey which takes a database-centric view of XML, [Widom, 1999]
noted that the concept of functional dependencies in the context of XML has
not been explored.

However, *keys,* which are a special case of functional dependencies, are
studied in the context of XML by [Buneman et al., 2001a]. It offers two basic
definitions for keys in XML : strong keys and weak keys. If a key is a strong
key, then given a set of elements, each element in the set must have a path
to the key node, and the value of the key node must be unique. If a key is a
weak key, then given a set of elements, for each element in the set, if there is a
path to the key node then the value of the key node must be unique. Consider
an XML document in which it is not mandatory for every person to have a
driving licence number but if they do, then the number is unique. The driving
licence number is then a weak key, but not a strong key. Weak key paths can be
missing, which makes weak keys similar to null-valued keys in the relational
context. [Buneman et al., 2001a] also noted that there are many other possible
definitions for keys, and introduced the concept of *relative keys.* Noting that
keys in many data formats (e.g. scientific databases) have a hierarchical structure, relative keys provide hierarchical key structures to accommodate such
databases. Consider an XML document that contains information about students enrolled in courses, assuming that a student can enroll in a course only
once then the student number is a key relative to the course. Such structures
are similar to the notion of ID dependent relationships in Entity Relationship
diagrams.

[Fan and Simeon, 2000] proposed constraint languages to capture semantics of XML documents using simply key, foreign key and inverse constraints.
However, functional dependencies, which form the theoretic foundation for
keys, were not addressed in these works.

The concept of allowing controlled data redundancy in exchange for faster
processing was introduced in [Ling et al., 1996]. In Chapter 7, we present
analogous arguments in the XML context for allowing controlled data redun-

dancy. Preliminary work has also been done on semantics preservation when translating data between the relational tables and XML [Lee and Chu, 2000].

Normal forms defined for relational databases, both 3NF, BCNF, 4NF and 5NF for the flat relational model, and nested relational normal forms like NNF [Ozsoyoglu and Yuan, 1987] and NF-NR [Ling and Yan, 1994] have been studied intensively in the past two decades. However, the above normal forms for traditional data models are not directly applicable to semistructured data for the following reasons. First, the semistructured data model is richer and more complex than the relational data model. For example, XML incorporates cardinality constraints that are not found in the relational data model. Second, in semistructured data, the schema is descriptive, rather than prescriptive. Hence no regular structure is expected in semistructured data instances.

We mentioned in this chapter that ORA-SS bears some similarity to nested relations, in that both have a tree-like structure and allow repeating groups or multiple occurrences of objects, and that such correspondence allows us to map an ORA-SS schema diagram to nested relations. However, ORA-SS is different from nested relations in the following significant ways: First, ORA-SS defines relationship types that are not available in nested relations. Second, reference is one of the four main concepts defined in ORA-SS schema diagrams, while it is represented using foreign keys in nested relations. These differences in the data models determine the differences in their normal form definition as well as their design methods.

The first work to investigate the problem of normalization in semistructured schemas is presented in [Lee et al., 1999]. It defines an S3-NF normal form for S3-Graph (or SemiStructured Schema Graph), which is basically a labeled graph in which vertices correspond to objects and edges represent the object-subobject relationships. Unlike the ORA-SS schema diagram, the S3-Graph is not able to model the semantics traditionally needed for recognizing redundancy in databases. For example, it cannot show the degree of an n-ary relationship type; neither can it distinguish between attributes of object classes and attributes of relationship types. To identify redundancy in an S3-Graph, [Lee et al., 1999] define a dependency constraint called SS-Dependency. An S3-Graph is in S3-NF if there is no transitive SS-dependency. Hence, only a limited kind of redundancy can be recognized by S3-NF. In [Lee et al., 1999], the authors present two approaches for designing S3-NF databases. One is a decomposition method, which can transform the schema to reduce redundancy based on SS-dependency. This decomposition may not always remove all transitive functional dependencies. The other method is to transform a normal form ER diagram [Lee et al., 1999] into an S3-Graph. Although the result obtained is in S3-NF, it is not unique and is dependent on the path taken to construct it.

Therefore, the result may not satisfy the application requirements or comply with the user's viewpoints.

In [Wu et al., 2001b], we propose a normal form for the semistructured schema called NF-SS, which extends S3-NF. NF-SS involves the XML model with integrity constraints, such as extended functional dependency (EFD) and key constraints. The NF-SS model improves on S3-Graphs by providing the notion of objects and attributes, and specifying cardinality on the schema. However, the NF-SS model still has no concept of composite attributes, and no distinction between relationship type attributes and object class attributes. A major difference between NF ORA-SS and NF-SS is that NF-SS does not deal with relationship types, as they are not available in its data model definition. A semistructured schema is in NF-SS, if it has no transitive or partial EFD and incoherent EFD. This is recursively defined by requiring the components of every object type (starting from the root and then proceeding downward) should not be transitively dependent on their parents, and should be as near to their owners as possible. Since the semantic information expressed by the data model is very limited, the NF-SS definition identifies redundancy mainly through the specified EFDs for the schema. In [Wu et al., 2001b], we propose a restructuring approach to design NF-SS. We develop an iterative algorithm based on a set of heuristic rules to restructure a semistructured schema into a normal form. The restructuring involves the decomposition of object types, creation of new object types and regrouping of components in a semistructured schema. The objective is to remove transitive or partial EFD and incoherent EFD, and is accomplished by identifying violations of the conditions of NF-SS given the dependency and key constraints. Similar to the decomposition methods for relational normalization, the NF-SS restructuring approach is not able to guarantee dependency covering or dependency preservation.

In [Embley and Mok, 2001], the authors propose a normal form for XML document called XNF (XML Normal Form). The process of generating an XNF-compliant DTD follows: it first takes a conceptual model-based methodology, using CM hypergraphs (conceptual-model hypergraphs), to model an application. Then it translates the CM hypergraph M to a scheme-tree forest F. F is in XNF if each scheme tree in F has no potential redundancy with respect to a specified set of (functional and multivalued) constraints C, and F has as few scheme trees as any other scheme-tree forest corresponding to M in which each scheme tree has no potential redundancy with respect to C. Finally, it generates a DTD from the scheme-tree. Like S3-Graph, CM hypergraph has no concept of attributes resulting in too many objects in a schema; in addition, CM hypergraph has no hierarchical structure. The algorithms for translating a CM hypergraph M to a scheme-tree forest are non-deterministic, and suffer from inefficiency. Additionally, adding or deleting required information requires a redesign of the whole schema. Further, the algorithms generate a large number of solutions rather than verifying whether a semistructured schema is in normal form or not. While the ISA relationship can be represented in CM hypergraphs, it is removed from CM hypergraph before input to the algorithm.

In [Arenas and Libkin, 2004], the authors show how to detect certain kinds of anomalies, and how to transform documents into ones that do not suffer from the same anomalies. They first introduce functional dependencies for XML by considering a relational representation of documents and defining functional dependencies on them, and later extend functional dependencies while considering functional dependencies in incomplete relations. They show that the normal form they define, called XNF, extends BCNF when limited to relational data. Many of the constraints while not being captured in the data model are captured in the definition of functional dependencies. Functional dependencies are already the area that designers have the most problem specifying in the relational model so making them more complicated and unfamiliar to designers will make the transition from the relational to the semistructured schema design more difficult. The functional dependencies are dependent on the XML Tree, including paths through the tree, so when paths change the functional dependencies change. For example to express the constraint that two distinct student elements of the same course cannot have the same *stuNo* in the XML document in Figure 5.1, we would write:

$$\{department.course, department.course.student.@stuNo\} \rightarrow$$
$$department.course.student.$$

For this reason XNF can never be dependency preserving. Also multivalued dependencies are not considered in XNF.

A common problem for the above normalization approaches is the following: the whole schema has to be redesigned when requirements change and information is added or deleted. Such approaches can be fairly inefficient for processing semistructured data, because the overhead of redesigning the whole schema structure can be substantial if the data structure is changing frequently.

The ORA-SS design approach presented in this chapter reduces the design complexity by facilitating the 2-level design technique. First, a designer identifies object classes and relationship types from the user's specifications. Then the designer adds attributes for object classes and relationship types. This 2-level design technique not only gives more control to the designer and allows him/her to evaluate each successive refinement of the schema, but also accommodates one of the central characteristics of semistructured data, namely its frequently changing structure [Abiteboul et al., 1999b].

Chapter 6

VIEWS

XML views are essential for managing XML data on the Web. Just like views in traditional databases, XML views provide application-specific views of the source data and secure the source data [Abiteboul, 1999].

Several systems have been proposed to support XML views. Systems such as SilkRoute [Fernandez et al., 2000] and XPERANTO [Carey et al., 2000] provide XML views over relational databases. Others such as Xyleme [Cluet et al., 2001] and ActiveView [Abiteboul et al., 1999a] allow the definition of XML views over native XML files. The ActiveView system [Abiteboul et al., 1999a] defines views using the object-oriented approach, which allows not only data, but also methods.

XML Views are also used as a middleware in data integration systems such as MIX [Baru et al., 1999] and MARS [Deutsch and Tannen, 2003]. The MIX system [Baru et al., 1999] integrates heterogeneous data sources and offers views based on the underlying data sources.

While existing systems provide for the definition of XML views, they do not validate the views that are created. Therefore, there is no guarantee that the views defined are valid.

Valid XML Views. Let V be a view defined over an XML data source D. V is said to be *valid* if it does not violate the semantics, that is, functional dependencies, relationship types and their degrees (binary, ternary and n-ary), and key and foreign key constraints implied in D.

In this chapter, we describe a systematic approach to ensure the validity of XML views. We have designed a set of rules to guide the design of valid XML views. Section 6.1 gives an example to illustrate the need for view validation. Sections 6.2 to 6.6 describe the various operators for designing views, and the rules for ensuring that the view obtained is valid, presents Section 6.7 discusses related work and we conclude in section 6.8.

6.1   Motivating Example

We will first illustrate the concept of valid and invalid views. Invalid views arise when important semantics are not expressed in the underlying data model.

Consider the following segment of an XML document on supplier, project and part *(spj.xml:*

$$< supplier \quad sno = "s001" \quad sname = "supplier01" >$$
$$< project \quad jno = "j001" \quad jname = "project01" >$$
$$< part \quad pno = "p001" \quad pname = "part01" >$$
$$< price > \ 100 < /price >$$
$$< qty > 200 < /qty >$$
$$< /part >$$
$$< /project >$$

$$< project \quad jno = "j002" \quad jname = "project02" >$$
$$< part \quad pno = "p002" \quad pname = "part02" >$$
$$< price > 150 < /price >$$
$$< qty > 300 < /qty >$$
$$< /part >$$
$$< /project >$$
$$< /supplier >$$

The following functional dependencies hold in the above XML document:

$$sno \rightarrow sname$$
$$jno \rightarrow jname$$
$$pno \rightarrow pname$$
$$sno, pno \rightarrow price$$
$$sno, pno, jno \rightarrow qty$$

The sub-element *price* denotes the price of its parent element *part* that is supplied by its ancestor element *supplier;* while the sub-element *qty* denotes the quantity of its parent element *part* supplied by its ancestor element *supplier* in its ancestor element *project.*

Figure 6.1 shows the ORA-SS schema of the XML document *spj.xml.* There are three object classes - *supplier, project* and *part.* Based on the functional dependencies implied in the XML document, the identifiers of supplier, project and part are *sno, jno* and *pno* respectively.

In addition, there are two relationship types in the ORA-SS schema. The first one is a binary relationship type between the object classes *supplier* and *part* which has been labeled as *sp(supplier, part)* on the incoming edge of the object class *part.* Note that the two participating object classes of the relation-

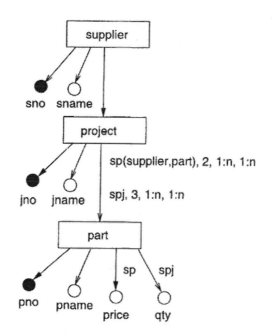

Figure 6.1. A Supplier-Part-Project ORA-SS Schema Diagram

ship type *sp* are not adjacent to each other in the root-to-leaf path in Figure 6.1. Hence, the names of the participating object classes are explicitly listed on the label of the edge.

The attribute *price* is a single-valued attribute of the relationship type *sp* because of the functional dependency:

$$sno, pno \rightarrow price$$

The second relationship type is a ternary relationship type *spj*, which involves the three object classes. It has a single-valued attribute *qty* because of the functional dependency:

$$sno, pno, jno \rightarrow qty$$

The semantics captured by the ORA-SS schema plays an important role in the design of valid XML views. The following shows the DTD of the XML document *spj.xml:*

```
<!ELEMENT supplies (supplier+) >
   <!ELEMENT supplier (project+) >
   <!ELEMENT project (part+) >
```

```
<!ELEMENT  part  (qty, price) >
<!ELEMENT  qty  (#PCDATA) >
<!ELEMENT  price  (#PCDATA) >

<!ATTLIST  supplier  sno  ID  #REQUIRED
             sname  CDATA  #REQUIRED >

<!ATTLIST  project  jno  #REQUIRED
             jname  CDATA  #REQUIRED >

<!ATTLIST  part  pno  #REQUIRED
             pname  CDATA  #REQUIRED >
```

Note that we cannot express *jno* and *pno* as the ID of the elements *supplier* and *part* respectively in the DTD. This is because these elements are involved in a many-to-many relationship with *project* and will occur multiple times in an XML document.

We observe that the elements *price* and *qty* are represented in the same manner as the elements *supplier* and *part*. In other words, the DTD cannot express the two functional dependencies:

$$sno, pno \rightarrow price$$
$$sno, pno, jno \rightarrow qty$$

Further, the DTD also cannot differentiate object class, attribute and relationship type.

Let us now design a view that swaps the hierarchical positions of the elements *project* and *part*. That is, *project* becomes a child of *part* and *part* becomes the parent of *project*. Obviously, the attributes *pno* and *pname* of the object class *part* will move up together with *part* since they are properties of *part*. Similarly, the attributes *jno* and *jname* of object class *project* will move down with *project*.

A possible view as shown in Figure 6.2 is created. Since the DTD XML does not explicitly express the functional dependencies involving *price* and *qty*, these elements have also moved up together with *part*. This is an invalid view because it violates the functional dependency in the source document:

$$sno, pno, jno \rightarrow qty$$

The problem of invalid view can be resolved by utilizing the ORA-SS model. Based on the ORA-SS source schema in Figure 6.1, we can design a valid view that swaps *project* and *part* (see Figure 6.3).

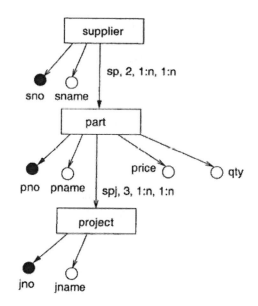

Figure 6.2. An Invalid XML View of the Supplier-Part-Project Schema in Figure 6.1

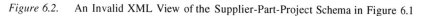

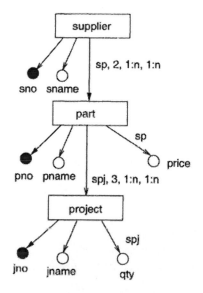

Figure 6.3. A Valid XML View of the Supplier-Part-Project Schema in Figure 6.1

The ORA-SS source schema explicitly expresses the functional dependencies involving *price* and *qty*. Thus, *price* will be placed under *part* and *qty* will be placed under *project* so that the original functional dependencies are preserved in the view.

We have demonstrated that invalid views may be wrongly created if the underlying data model does not explicitly express the necessary semantics, namely, functional dependencies, relationship types and their degrees (binary, ternary or n-ary), and key and foreign key constraints. Such semantics are not captured by the DTD or XML Schema. Thus, we cannot determine whether an XML view is valid or not based on a DTD or XML Schema. However, the ORA-SS model can explicitly express all these semantics, which allows us to determine if an XML view is valid or not.

In the following sections, we will give more details on how to design valid XML views based on ORA-SS. The XML views considered are created by applying four transformation operations on the source ORA-SS schema. The operations are select, drop, join and swap. The select and join operations are analogous to the select and join operations in relational database. The drop operation is the opposite of the project operation in relational database. The fourth operation swap is unique in XML; it interchanges the positions of parent and child object classes. An XML view can be created via a composition of the four operations, that is, a view may first apply a selection operation followed by a join operation, etc. We have developed a set of rules for each operator to guarantee the validity of XML views when any of the four operations is applied.

6.2   The Select Operator

Selection operations are commonly used to filter data by using predicates. They are similar to the selection operators in relational databases. The structure of the source schema remains unchanged and will not cause any changes in the semantics or the hierarchical structure of the source schema. Therefore, if an XML view only applies selection operations, it will always be valid. This operation is also supported in the Active Views system and MIX system.

Example 6.1 *Suppose we want to design a view called expensive-supplier on the ORA-SS source schema diagram in Figure 6.1 that returns the suppliers who supply some project with part and the price of the part is greater than 80. Figure 6.4 shows the view with a selection predicate on the attribute price.*

In general, selection operations place predicates on the source schema, which filter out data that do not satisfy those predicates. They do not restructure the source document and thus, will not lead to any violation of semantics in the source schema. Therefore, there is no need to set up rules to guarantee the validity of views for selection operations. In fact, one can easily design such views using some simple data models such as OEM or XML DTD.

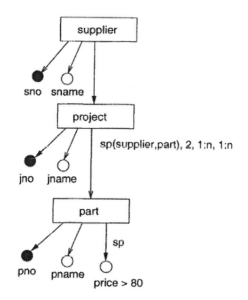

Figure 6.4. An XML View of the Supplier-Part-Project Schema in Figure 6.1 obtained by the Selection Operator

6.3   The Drop Operator

The drop operation drops object classes or attributes in the source schema. It essentially extracts a subset of the structure of the source schema. When an object class is dropped, it may be because the object class itself is dropped, or because the identifier of the object class is dropped. When a projection operation drops object classes or attributes in the source schema, it affects relationship types involving the dropped object class. In another words, the semantics of the source schema will be affected.

The following example illustrates the case where a projection operator is applied.

Example 6.2 *Suppose we define a view called project-part on the ORA-SS schema diagram in Figure 6.1. This view removes the object class supplier (see Figure 6.5). This implies that all the attributes of supplier, namely, sno and sname, have to be dropped since object attributes cannot exist without its owner object class.*

We also need to remove the relationship types sp and spj, both of which involves the object class supplier that has been dropped. These two relationship types will not exist in the view schema. In addition, the attribute of the relationship type sp, that is, price, is also dropped from the view schema.

The attribute qty of the relationship type spj can be mapped to an aggregate attribute called total-qty, which represents the total quantity of a part in a

118

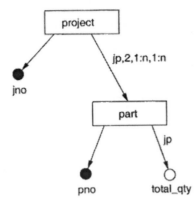

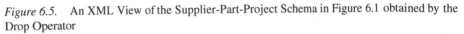

Figure 6.5. An XML View of the Supplier-Part-Project Schema in Figure 6.1 obtained by the Drop Operator

given project. In other words, it is an attribute of a new relationship type involving project and part, which is derived from spj.

The above example shows that flexible views can be designed based on ORA-SS with its additional semantics. However, we have to handle the semantics properly so that valid views are guaranteed. This example also implies the following four rules that guarantee the validity of XML views when projection operations are applied.

Rule Drop1. *If an object class O in a source schema is dropped from a view, then all the attributes of O must be dropped from the view too.*

Rule Drop2. *If an object class O in a source schema is dropped from a view, then all the relationship types that the object class is involved in must be dropped from the view too.*

Rule Drop3. *If an object class O in a source schema is dropped from a view, then for each n-ary (n ≥ 2) relationship type R involving O, a new relationship type is generated by projecting R on the dropped object class O. The attributes of R can be dropped, or mapped into attributes with aggregate function, such as avg, max/min or sum. Alternatively, the attributes of R can be mapped into an attribute of type bag of values if they cannot be aggregated.*

Rule Drop4. *Let an object class O in a source schema be dropped from a view. Suppose the following conditions are true:*

 1 *O is the only common participating object class of two relationship types R1 and R2;*

2 *All the participating object classes of R1 and R2 are in a continual path;*

3 *The participating object classes of R1 is not a subset of the participating object classes of R2 and vice versa.*

Then a new relationship type can be obtained by joining R1 and R2 based on the object class O.

We will now discuss each of the four rules in details and demonstrate why they are able to guarantee the validity of XML views.

RULE DROP1

Intuitively, Rule Drop1 indicates that we cannot leave an attribute in the view if its owner object class has been dropped from the view. Without their object class, the attributes will lose their meaning.

RULE DROP2

Rule Drop2 handles the situation when one participating object class of a relationship type is dropped in the view, in which case the relationship type is broken up. Although the relationship type will not be shown in an XML document or an XML schema, it needs to be dropped to keep the semantics in the ORA-SS view schema consistent.

After a relationship type has been dropped, the rest of the object classes involved in the relationship type still have semantic connections in the view. In order to maintain these semantic connection in the view, we can derive a new relationship type from the relationship type that has been dropped. This gives us the Rule Drop3.

RULE DROP3

Suppose object classes $O_1, O_2, ..., O_n$ participate in a relationship type R in a source schema. Let us assume that one of the object classes, say $O_i, 1 \leq i \leq n$, is dropped from a view. According to Rule Proj3, a new relationship type R' can be derived from R by projecting out O_i and all the attributes of R, that is, all the object classes of R except for O_i are kept in the new relationship type R'.

It is clear that R' will not violate the semantics implied in R according to the theory of relational database. Instead, it is able to maintain the semantic connection among the object classes in the view.

The attributes of R can be dropped from the view. Alternatively, new attributes can be derived according to the Rule Drop3. The new derived attributes remain valid in the view schema.

This approach correctly maintains the semantics among the remaining object classes of the relationship type R.

RULE DROP4

The above three rules are not sufficient when the object class that has been dropped from the view is involved in more than one relationship type in the source schema. In such situations, we need to join these relationship types in order to maintain the semantic connection among them.

Rule Drop4 contains additional conditions besides the project operator itself. We will show why these conditions are important.

Let us assume that the first condition does not hold, that is, R1 and R2 have other common object classes. In this case, it is clear that we do not have to join R1 and R2 since the semantic connection between R1 and R2 is still explicitly expressed through the other common object classes.

Next, suppose the second condition is false, that is, all the participating object classes of R1 and R2 do not lie in the same path. In this case, we cannot join R1 and R2 since the object classes of the new relationship type will not be in the same path, and the new relationship type will be meaningless.

Finally, suppose that the third condition is false. Then either all participating object classes of R1 participate in R2 or vice versa. In this situation, if the only common object class of R1 and R2 is dropped, then all the object classes of R1 must have been removed in the view schema. Thus, we do not need to join R1 and R2 in the view schema.

The view designed using Rule Drop4 is valid. Suppose object classes O_{11}, $O_{12}, ..., O_{1n}$ participate in the relationship type Rl in the order from ancestor to descendant, and object class $O_{21}, O_{22}, ..., O_{2m}$ participate in the relationship type R2 in the order from ancestor to descendant in the source schema. Then the relationship types R1 and R2 are in the same path in the schema, and they do not contain each other. Suppose that O_{1n} and O_{21} are the same object class and this object class is the only object class that is common to R1 and R2, and this object class is dropped from the view.

Since all the conditions in Rule Drop4 are satisfied, we can derive a new relationship type R' in the view schema by joining R1 and R2. Obviously, the derived relationship type R' maintains the semantic connection among the two relationship types, and does not violate the semantics of R1 and R2 according to the theory of relational database. Therefore, the semantics among the remaining object classes that participate in R1 and R2 in the view is correctly kept and the view is valid.

The following example illustrates how Rule Drop4 is applied to ensure the validity of a view.

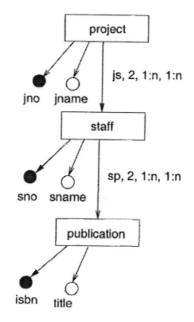

Figure 6.6. ORA-SS source schema involving Project, Staff and Publication.

Example 6.3 *Figure 6.6 shows an ORA-SS source schema involving the object classes project, staff and publication. There is a binary relationship type called js involving the object classes project and staff. This relationship type captures the staff that participates in a project. The binary relationship type sp between staff and publication indicates the publications that a staff publishes.*

Figure 6.7 shows an ambiguous view that has been designed based on Figure 6.6. The intermediate object class staff has been dropped from this view. However, it is not clear how the view is derived from the source schema. We observe that the semantic connection between the two object classes project and publication has been lost.

In fact, we should maintain the semantic connection between project and publication to depict the publications that are published by the staff involved in a given project. Rule Drop4 states that we need to generate a new relationship type jp between the two object classes in the view, in order to ensure that the view is valid and meaningful (see Figure 6.8). The relationship type jp is derived by joining the relationship types js and sp over the object class staff in the source schema in Figure 6.6.

6.4 The Join Operator

ORA-SS makes it possible to create XML views by applying join operations and guarantee they are valid. This is because ORA-SS distinguishes between

122

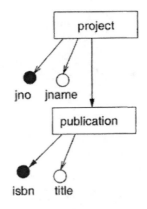

Figure 6.7. An ambiguous view of Figure 6.6.

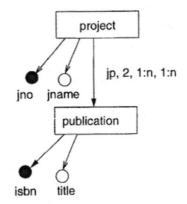

Figure 6.8. A valid view of Figure 6.6. The new relationship type *jp* is derived by joining *js* and *sp*.

object classes and attributes so that two object classes can be joined. Furthermore, ORA-SS differentiates between attributes of object classes and attributes of relationship types so that attributes of relationship types will not be treated as attributes of the joined object class improperly. These features of ORA-SS are not offered by other existing semistructured data model, which will not allow the design of such views.

A standard join operation joins object classes and their attributes together by key - foreign key references. Referencing object classes and referenced object classs may occur in an ORA-SS source diagram or in two ORA-SS source diagrams. The former has an attribute that is actually the OID of the latter object class. Therefore, the former is able to refer to the latter by the attribute, which plays the role of a foreign key.

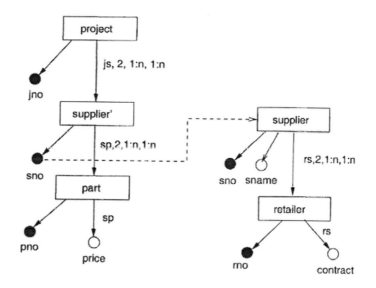

Figure 6.9. ORA-SS schema diagram on Project, Supplier, Part and Retailer

When a join operator is applied to an ORA-SS source schema to create a view, we will remove the referenced object class from the view schema and attach all attributes of the referenced object class to the referencing object class.

Example 6.4 *Figure 6.9 shows an ORA-SS source schema diagram. The object class supplier' under project refers to an object class supplier with the identifier of supplier. There is a relationship type called rs between supplier and retailer. This relationship type has an attribute called contract that is connected to retailer.*

Suppose we want to design a view called join-supplier, which applies a join operator to join supplier and supplier' together. Figure 6.10 shows the view schema in which the object class supplier has been removed, and the attributes sno and sname of supplier have been connected to supplier'. Further, the object class retailer has moved to below supplier', together with the attribute contract. Thus, the relationship type rs is maintained in the view.

The above example demonstrates that when a join operator is applied, we need to handle the object classes and relationship types in the path of the referenced object class.

We develop two rules to ensure the validity of views when a join operation is carried out. The first rule handles the descendants of the referenced object class and their relationship types. The second rule then handles the ancestors

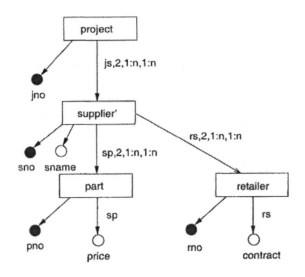

Figure 6.10. View of Figure 6.9 obtained by a join operation

of the referenced object class and their relationship types.

Rule Join1. *If a referencing object classes O_i is joined with a referenced object class O_j in the design of a view, then all attributes of O_j are attached to O_i in the view. If there is a relationship type R which does not involve any ancestors of O_j but only involves the descendants of O_j, then*

Case 1: *Keep R and all its participating object classes in the view.*

Case 2: *Drop some of the object classes of R in the view to derive a new relationship type. The attributes of R can either be dropped, mapped into attributes with some aggregate function.*

Rule Join1 first attaches the attributes of O_j to O_i since O_i refers to O_j by a foreign key to key reference and O_i plays the role of O_j in the view. Next, Rule Join1 handles the relationship types involving the descendants of O_j in the view. There are two possible scenarios. Suppose one of the relationship types is R. In Case 1, R is kept in the view. Thus, all the participating object classes of R are also kept in the view and O_i plays the role of O_j in R. It is clear that the semantics of R is maintained in the view and the view is valid.

In Case 2, a new relationship type is derived from R by dropping some of the participating object classes of R. The attributes of R can also be handled properly based on users' requirements. According to Rule Drop3, the new relationship type will not violate the semantics of R and the view is thus valid.

On the other hand, we also need to handle the ancestors of O_j in the source schema and their relationship types, especially when the ancestors of O_j participates in a relationship type with O_j or its descendants. Rule Join2 handles this situation.

Rule Join2. *If a referencing object class O_i is joined with a referenced object class O_j in designing a view, then all the attributes of O_j are attached to O_i in the view. If there is a relationship type R involving the ancestors of O_j, then*

    Case 1: *Keep R in the view and swap the ancestors of O_j involving R below O_j.*

    Case 2: *Drop the ancestors of O_j involving R in the view to derive a new relationship type. The attributes of R can be dropped or mapped into attributes with some aggregate function.*

Rule Join2 handles the relationship types that involve the ancestors of O_j in the view. There are two possible cases when processing these relationship types. Suppose one of the relationship types is R. In Case 1, R and the ancestors of O_j participating in R are needed in the view schema. Thus, the ancestors must be swapped first and become the descendants of O_j so that they can be attached as O_i's descendants in the view schema. In this way, R is kept intact in the view and the view is still valid. Notice a new operator, i.e. swap operator is utilized in this case. More details on the swap operator will be given in the following section.

In Case 2, we simply drop all the ancestors of O_j involving R in the view. As the ancestors of O_i are already in the view, the ancestors of O_j in the source schema cannot appear as ancestors of O_i in the view. After dropping these ancestors, a new relationship type can be derived from R and the attributes can be handled properly in the view schema. In this way, we can ensure that the view designed will be valid.

6.5 The Swap Operator

The swap operation restructures the source schema by exchanging the positions of a parent object class and its child object class. Swap operations are unique in XML because they can be applied only in hierarchical structure. Further, the swap operator also raises the issue of view reversibility. That is, when we swap two object classes to construct a view schema, we can reconstruct the original source schema from the view by carrying out a reverse swapping. Therefore, we require not only rules to design valid views, but also rules to guarantee that the designed views are reversible.

126

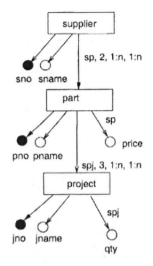

Figure 6.11. ORA-SS schema of Supplier-Part-Project

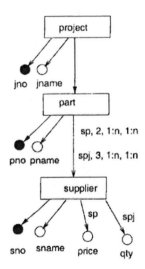

Figure 6.12. View of Figure 6.11 obtained by a swap operation

The following example illustrates how to design valid XML views when the swap operation is applied.

Example 6.5 *Figure 6.11 shows a source schema involving the object classes supplier, part and project. Suppose we want to design a view called swap-supplier-project, that swaps the object classes supplier and project hierarchically. Figure 6.12 shows the view obtained.*

After the object classes supplier and project have been swapped, we need to ensure that their attributes are relocated properly.

It is clear that the attributes sno and sname should move together with their owner object class supplier. Likewise, the attributes jno and jname should move together with their owner object class project. However, the attribute price, which belongs to the relationship type sp, must remain with the new child object class of sp, that is, supplier in order to preserve the semantics of the source schema, that is, the functional dependency

$$sno, pno \rightarrow price$$

If the attribute price remains with the object class part, then it will violate the functional dependency in the source schema.

Similarly, the attribute qty of the relationship type spj is connected to the lowest participating object class of spj, that is, supplier.

We will now examine the rules that guarantee the validity of views when swap operations are applied.

Rule Swap1. If a view swaps two object classes O_i and O_j, where O_j is a descendant of O_i in the source schema, then the attributes of O_i and O_j must remain attached to O_i and O_j respectively in the view.

Rule Swap 1 is straightforward and ensures that the attributes of O_i and O_j do not become meaningless in the view after O_i and O_j has been swapped.

We observe that relationship types in the source schema that involve O_i and/or O_j are affected since the hierarchical positions of O_i and O_j have been interchanged. Given two object classes O_i and O_j where O_j is a descendant of O_i in an ORA-SS schema, the relationship types that are affected after a swap of O_i and O_j can be classified into the following three categories:

- The first category is the set of relationship types which do not involve any descendants of O_j, but involve the ancestors of O_i or O_j in the ORA-SS source schema. That is, these relationship type involve object classes that occur in the straight path of O_i and O_j (up to O_j).

- The second category is the set of relationship types which involve O_i and object classes in the branch paths between O_i and the parent of O_j.

- The third category is the set of relationship types which involve O_j and its descendants.

These three categories of affected relationship types are handled by the rules Swap2, Swap3 and Swap4 respectively.

Rule Swap2. Suppose two object classes O_i and O_j in a source schema are swapped during the design of a view. Let S be the set of relationship types which do not involve any descendants of O_j, but involve the ancestors of O_i or O_j in the ORA-SS source schema. For each relationship type R in S, the attributes of R are attached to the lowest participating object class of R in the view.

Rule Swap3 Suppose an object class O_i in a source schema is swapped with its descendant object class O_j during the design of a view. If there exists a relationship type which involves at least O_i and O_c, where O_c is a descendant of an object class O_a that lies in the path between O_i and O_j, but O_c does not lie in the path between O_i and O_j in the ORA-SS source schema, then the subtree rooted at O_c is attached to O_i in the view.

Rule Swap4 Suppose an object class O_i in a source schema is swapped with its descendant object class O_j during the design of a view. For each child O_d of the object class O_j, let T be the subtree that is rooted at O_d. Let S be the set of relationship types which involve at least O_j and its descendants in T. If O_l is the lowest participating object class among the relationship types in S that lie in the path between O_i and O_j *after* the swap, then the subtree rooted at O_d is O_l.

Example 6.6 *Figure 6.13 shows the relationship types in an ORA-SS source schema that will be affected when object classes O_i and O_j are swapped. The relationship type R_1 involves the ancestors of O_i and/or O_j. All the object classes of any such relationship type R_1 will remain in the same path after O_i and O_j are swapped. However, the lowest participating object class of R_1 may be changed, and Rule Swap2 will attach any attributes of R_1 to the new lowest participating object class of R_1 in the view. In this way, the view will not violate the semantics in the source schema and is valid. Note that the relationship type R_1 does not involve O_j's descendants since the relationship type will not be affected by the swap.*

The relationship types R_2 and R_3 in Figure 6.13 involve object classes in the branch paths of O_i and O_j. R_2 involves O_i and its child O_c, where O_c does not lie in the path between O_i and O_j, while R_3 involves O_i, O_a and O_b, where O_a lies in the path between O_i and O_j but O_b does not. When O_i and O_j are swapped, the subtrees rooted at O_b and O_c need to be attached to O_i so that the semantics of R_2 and R_3 remain intact, and the view obtained after the swap is still valid.

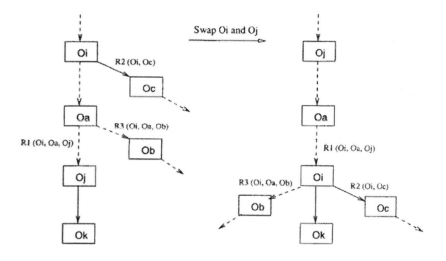

Figure 6.13. Handling relationship types that are affected by a swap operation.

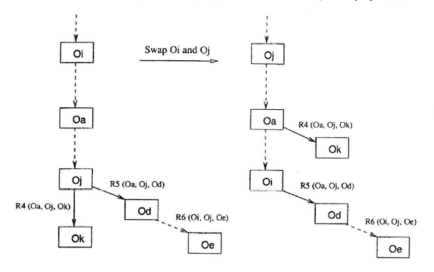

Figure 6.14. Handling relationship types that involve the descendants of O_j.

Example 6.7 *Figure 6.14 shows how relationship types that involve the descendants of O_j are handled after a swap operation. O_j has two children, namely O_k and O_d. The relationship type R_4 involves O_j and O_k. Since O_j is the lowest participating object class of R_4 after the swap, the subtree that is rooted at O_k remains attached to O_j. In contrast, the subtree that is rooted at O_d has two relationship types R_5 and R_6. Since O_i is the lowest participating object class among all the participating object classes in R_5 and R_6 after the swap, the subtree that is rooted at O_d is attached to O_i.*

In general, if a relationship type does not involve any ancestors of O_j but only the descendants of O_j, then the subtree rooted at O_d remains attached to O_j since O_j is the lowest participating object class of R in the view. However, if R involve some ancestors of O_j, then the subtree rooted at O_d will be attached to the lowest participating object class of R in the view so that the semantics of R remain intact.

Reversible Views

A valid view schema V of a source schema S is a *reversible view* if the source schema is a valid view of V after the application of any of the view operator, i.e., select, drop, join or swap).

If the original source schema can be obtained back by applying some operators to a view, we say that the view is reversible. Among the four view operators, it is obvious that the select and drop operators will not yield a reversible view. This is because some data will be lost in the view, and it is impossible to recover the data back from the view. The join operator connects two object classes together, and from the rules for the join operator, the source data may not be lost in the view. However, we will need to introduce new operators to restore the referenced object class if we want the view to be reversible, which is beyond the scope here. Finally, the swap operator interchanges two object classes in the view which is reversible when another swap operation is applied.

The following example illustrates the reversible view problem. It also shows that an invalid view may be produced if we do not apply rules Swap3 and Swap4.

Example 6.8 *Suppose we have the source schema as shown in Figure 6.15, and we want to design a view that swaps the object classes course and student. Based on the rules Swap1 and Swap2, we first move the attributes of the two object classes together with their owner object classes, and the relationship type cs's attribute grade is attached to course, that is, the new lowest participating object class of cs.*

Note that the participating object classes in the relationship dc has to be explicitly stated as dc(department, course), 2, 1:n, 1:1. This is because these two object classes are not located next to each other in the path. There is an object class student between them in the same path. If the participating object classes of the relationship dc is not specified, the default participating object classes will be student and course.

Figure 6.15 also has a relationship type called dcl that involves department, course and lecturer. If we do not have Rule Swap3, then the object class lecturer will be attached to student in the view and the relationship type dcl

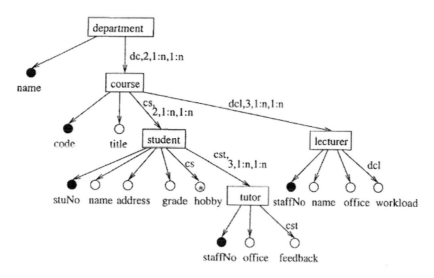

Figure 6.15. ORA-SS schema of course-student-lecturer

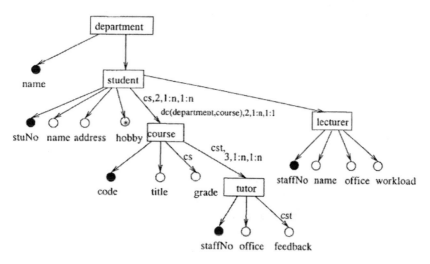

Figure 6.16. An invalid view of Figure 6.15 after swapping *student* and *course*

will be lost in the view (see Figure 6.16). Thus, all the distinct lecturers will be repeatedly placed under each student in the corresponding XML view documents. Further, the attribute workload will become meaningless as it wrongly becomes an attribute of lecturer in the view. The view in Figure 6.16 is invalid.

In order to obtain a valid view as shown in Figure 6.17, the object class lecturer needs to move down with course to keep the semantics of the relationship type dcl intact. We also need to explicitly indicate the participating object classes of dcl since they are not adjacent to each other in the view. The

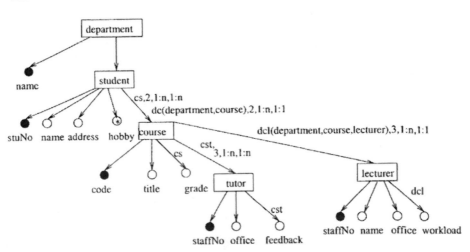

Figure 6.17. A valid reversible view of Figure 6.15 after swapping *student* and *course*

meaning of the attribute workload is still the same as in the source schema, that is, the workload of a lecturer under a given pair of course and department,

Note that we do not need to move the object class tutor up with student although tutor and student are involved in the relationship type cst. This is because, based on Rule Swap4, tutor needs to be attached to the lowest participating object class of cst, i.e., course. Thus, the semantics of the ternary relationship type cst remains unchanged and the resulting view in Figure 6.17 is valid and reversible.

Let us now apply another swap operator to the view in Figure 6.17 to swap student and course. Applying the rules Swap1 and Swap2, the attributes of student and course will move together with their owner object classes. The relationship attribute grade is thus attached to the object class student again. In addition, the object class lecturer will move up with course as a whole to keep the semantics of the relationship type dcl intact (Rule Swap4). The view obtained will be the same as the original source schema in Figure 6.15.

6.6 Design Rules for IDentifier Dependency Relationship

In the previous sections, we have presented the design rules when drop, join and swap operations are applied in XML views. However, these rules are not sufficient when the views contain *IDD (IDentifier Dependency)* relationship types. An *IDD* relationship type is defined as follows:

Definition 6.1 *An object class A is said to be ID dependent on its parent object class B if A does not have an identifier, and an A object can be identified by its parent's identifier value (say k1) together with some of its own attributes (say*

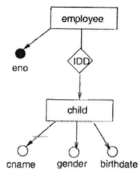

Figure 6.18. ORA-SS schema containing an IDD relationship type

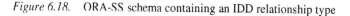
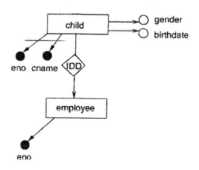

Figure 6.19. ORA-SS schema of a view that swaps employee and child

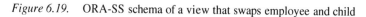
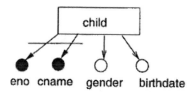

Figure 6.20. ORA-SS schema of a view that drops employee

k2). That is, the identifier of A is k1, k2. The relationship type between A and B is then called IDD relationship type.

Example 6.9 *Figure 6.18 shows an IDD relationship type between the object class employee and child. The object class child does not have a identifier, but can be identified by the identifier of employee, i.e., eno and its own attribute, i.e., cname. Thus, we have*

$$eno, cname \rightarrow gender, birthdate$$

When we design a view over the IDD relationship type, additional rules are needed to keep the view meaningful.

Based on Figure 6.18, we use the swap operation to design a view. Figure 6.19 shows that the object classes employee and child have been swapped. Note that this view duplicates the identifier of employee, i.e., eno for the object class child so that eno and cname combine to form an identifier for the object class child. This is because the object class child cannot be identified without eno. Note this view needs to be enforced with a constraint, which says the eno under the object class child must be the same as the eno under the object class employee. The straight line between the incoming edges of the attributes eno and cname denotes that eno, cname is a composite identifier for the object class child.

We can also design a view by applying the drop operation. Figure 6.20 depicts a view that drops the object class employee. In order to make the object class child identifiable, the identifier of employee, i.e., eno is also combined with the attribute cname to construct a identifier for the object class child.

A similar situation is obtained if a join operation is applied in a source schema containing an IDD relationship type.

The above example shows that when we design a view that destroys an IDD relationship type, the identifier of the parent object class of the IDD relationship type should be added to the child object class to construct a identifier for the child. The following additional rules specify how XML views should be designed when IDD relationship types are involved.

Rule IDD. If an IDD relationship type is destroyed when some view operator is applied, and the child object class of the IDD relationship type remains in the view, then the identifier of the parent object class is added to the weak identifier of the child object class to construct a identifier for the child object class.

6.7 Example of Designing View

Finally, we will illustrate how a valid view can be designed by utilizing the four view operators that we have discussed in the previous sections.

Example 6.10 *Let us design a view based on the ORA-SS source schema shown in Figure 6.21. The source schema shows a foreign key to key reference from the object class project' to project. There is also an IDD relationship type between the object classes employee and child.*

We first apply a join operator to join the object classes project' and project. Next, we apply a drop operator to drop the object class supplier. The view obtained after applying these two operators is shown in Figure 6.22.

Next, we apply a swap operator to swap the object classes part and project'. Since there is a relationship type between the object class part and factory, we need to move factory down together with part (Rule Swap3) to ensure that the

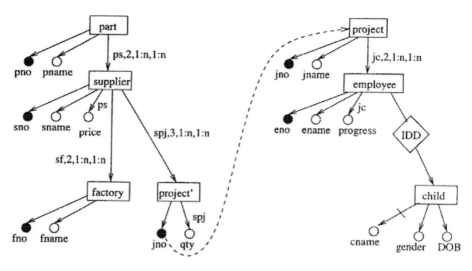

Figure 6.21. Example ORA-SS schema

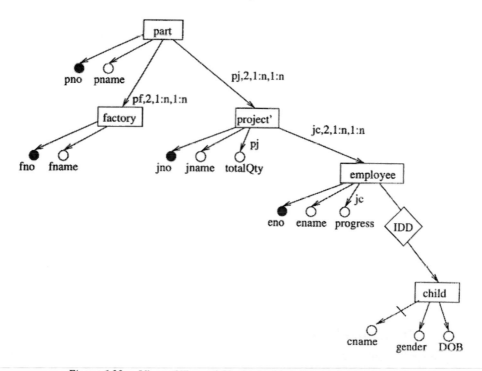

Figure 6.22. View of Figure 6.21 obtained by a join and a drop operator

resulting view is reversible (see Figure 6.23). Note that the object classes part and employee are not adjacent to each other in the view. Thus, we need to

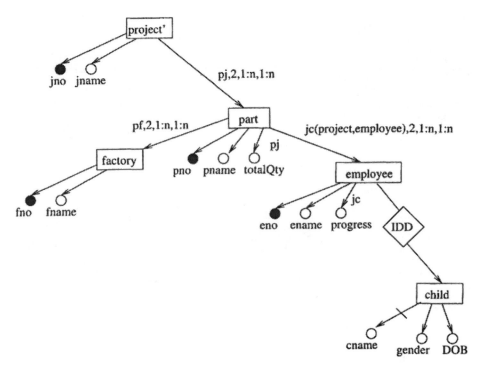

Figure 6.23. View obtained by swapping *part* and *project'* in Figure 6.22

explicitly indicate the two participating object classes for the relationship type
je.

Finally, we apply another swap operator to swap the object classes employee and child. From the Rule IDD, the attribute eno must be attached to the
object class child to construct an identifier for child. In addition, we also apply
a select operator to the attribute totalQty, i.e., "totalQty > 300". This gives us
a view that retrieves the pairs of project and part in which the project uses a
total of more than 300 of the part. Figure 6.24 depicts the final view.

6.8   Related Work

Several prototype systems have been developed to support the design of
XML views. The Active View system [Abiteboul et al., 1999a] is built on top
of Ardent Software's XML repository, which is based on the object-oriented
O2 system. In the Active Views system, a view is presented as an object, which
allows not only data, but also methods. The Active Views system uses XML
documents as its data model, which can only support views that apply selection

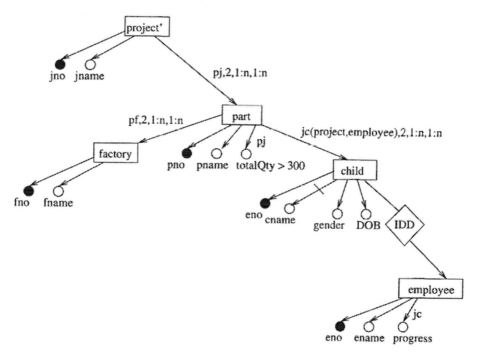

Figure 6.24. View obtained by swapping *employee* and *child* in Figure 6.23

operations. Projection, join and swap operations may be applied, but there is no guarantee that valid views are created.

MIX (Mediation of Information using XML) [Baru et al., 1999] is another system that offers a virtual XML view on its underlying heterogeneous sources. MIX utilizes DTD as its data model. Similar to XML document, XML DTD cannot express necessary semantics for valid XML view design, and their views can only support selection operations.

In contrast, our approach uses the ORA-SS data model to express both the source and view schemas. This allows us to support a richer set of views compared to Active Views and MIX. The Active Views system uses the Object Query Language as a view definition language, and the Lorel language as its query language over the views. This requires the users to be familiar with two different languages. MIX develops its own XMAS language as the view definition language and query language. In contrast, our approach directly adopts the W3C standard, XQuery as the query/view language over the views. A view definition is differentiated from a query by its additional view declaration clause before FLWR expression. Finally, both the Active Views system and MIX system do not provide for the validation of views. As a consequence, these two systems cannot guarantee valid XML views that apply projection, join and swap operations.

6.9   Summary

In this paper, we have proposed a systematic approach for valid XML view design. The approach is composed of three steps. The first step transforms an XML document into an ORA-SS schema diagram. The second step enriches the ORA-SS schema diagram with necessary semantics for valid XML views design. The final step uses the proposed a set of rules to guide the design of valid XML views. We have also presented rules to validate views.

Chapter 7

PHYSICAL DATABASE DESIGN

Until now, we have discussed the importance of designing good conceptual schema for semistructured databases. In practice, physical database design is the most important step when designing a schema since it affects the performance of the database system, in particular, the evaluation of queries. [Ling et al., 1996] advocates that logical and physical design steps should be integrated to guide the design of more "efficient" schemas while maintaining the integrity of the database.

One important aspect of physical database design is the controlled replication of data to provide more efficient data access. The benefit of replicating data is that the speed of queries may improve. The disadvantage is that inserting, deleting and maintaining data becomes more difficult, and that extra space is required for the storage of the data.

This chapter first reviews the physical database design concepts in the relational and hierarchical models. Then we will discuss how to apply related concepts when designing the physical schemas for XML documents.

7.1 Relational Database Physical Design

The core of relational database theory is functional dependencies and normalization. Normalization is a process that considers the functional dependencies between attributes and decides which attributes belong together in a relation. The result is a logical database design that is structurally consistent and has minimal redundancy. However, a normalized database design may not provide the optimal processing efficiency. This leads to the notion of *denormalization* whereby the relational schema is refined by introducing redundancy in a controlled manner to improve the performance of the database system.

Many steps can be taken in the physical design of relational databases. These include adding redundant columns, adding derived columns, collapsing tables, splitting tables both horizontally and vertically. However, the amount of redundancy, if not controlled, will lead to potential inconsistency or update anomalies. To overcome the problem of update anomalies, [Ling et al., 1996] extended classical functional dependencies (FDs) to include *strong* FDs.

An FD $X \rightarrow Y$ in a relation R is a *strong* FD, denoted by $X \xrightarrow{s} Y$ if all the attributes in Y will not be updates, or if the update need not be performed in real-time or online.

For example, the FDs *code* $\rightarrow$ *title* and *stuNo* $\rightarrow$ *name* are strong FDs.

Based on the notion of strong FD, [Ling et al., 1996] defined *replicated 3NF*, which allows some redundancies in a relation scheme so that the performance of the database system is improved while ensuring that the integrity of the database is not compromised due to various updating anomalies. This is accomplished by ensuring that

1 Only attributes that are rarely updated or attributes that can be updated off-line are duplicated. This is enforced by the definition of the strong FD.

2 Insertion, deletion, and updating anomalies cannot occur by adhering to a strict updating policy which will validate the updates against the primary instance of the attribute.

Definition 7.1 *[Ling et al., 1996] Let $R = \{R_1, R_2, ..., R_n\}$ be a relational database schema and let A_j be the set of attributes in R_j, for $j = 1, 2, ..., n$. A relation schema $R_i \in R$ is said to be in* **replicated 3NF** *if:*

1 For each $X \xrightarrow{s} Y$, $X \cup Y \subseteq A_i$, X is not a key of R_i.

    Case 1: *If X is not a role name of the key of R_i, then there exists a unique $R_j \in R, j \neq i$, such that X is a key of R_j and $Y \subset A_j$ (R_j is said to be the primary instance of R_i with respect to the attributes in $X \cup Y$).*

    Case 2: *If X is a role name of the key of R_i and Y is a role name of some attribute in R_i.*

2 Let $\beta = \{B | X \xrightarrow{s} B, \{X, B\} \subseteq A_i$, X is not a key of R_i, and B is non-prime\}; the relation schema obtained from R_i after removing all attributes in β is in 3NF.

Example 7.1 *Consider the following database schema where the keys of the relations are underlined:*

    SUPPLIER (<u>sno</u>, sname, addr)
    PART (<u>pno</u>, pname, color)
    SUPPLY (<u>sno, pno</u>, sname, pname, qty)

The relation SUPPLY is not in Codd 3NF (in fact, it is not in 2NF) because we have sno → sname but sname is non-prime and sno is not a candidate key, and sname is not fully functionally dependent on the key {sno,pno} of the SUPPLY relation. However, it is in replicated 3NF by Definition 1 since:

1 *we have sno $\xrightarrow{s}$ sname and pno $\xrightarrow{s}$ pname as we do not or seldom change the names of suppliers and the names of parts. By Case 1 of Definition 1, SUPPLIER and PART are the primary instances of SUPPLY with respect to the attribute sets {sno, sname} and {pno, pname} respectively; and*

2 $\beta = \{sname, pname\}$ *and the relation schema obtained by removing the attributes sname and pname from SUPPLY is in Codd 3NF.*

The replicated normal form provides for inclusion of redundancies in a relation scheme so that the operational efficiency of the database can be enhanced while ensuring that the integrity of the database is not compromised due to various updating anomalies.

This is achieved by ensuring that only attributes that are rarely updated or attributes that can be updated off-line are duplicated. This is enforced by the definition of a strong FD and the second condition of Definition 1.

Therefore, in our example scheme, we need to enforce the following inclusion dependencies:

$$\text{SUPPLY[sno, sname]} \subseteq \text{SUPPLIER [sno, sname]}$$
$$\text{SUPPLY[pno, pname]} \subseteq \text{PART [pno, pname]}$$

The strong FD and replicated 3NF provides the link between the logical and physical database design steps by allowing the database designer to make more informed decisions about how the physical database can be structured (by adding redundant attributes) without compromising the data integrity achieved during the logical design step while giving better retrieval performance.

7.2 IMS Database Physical Design

Pre-relational database systems such as the IBM's Information Management System or IMS [Date, 1975] is based on the hierarchical model. A student that takes a set of courses will be modeled in an IMS hierarchy in which student "parent segments" have subordinate course "child segments" (see Figure 7.1). Such hierarchies are efficient to answer queries such as "Retrieve the courses taken by some student John".

However this design leads to redundancy in the course segments. Information on a course that is taken by many students will be repeated. In order to remove redundant data in the course segments, IMS uses logical parent point-

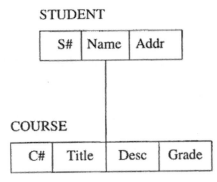

STUDENT

COURSE

Figure 7.1. Database design using IMS

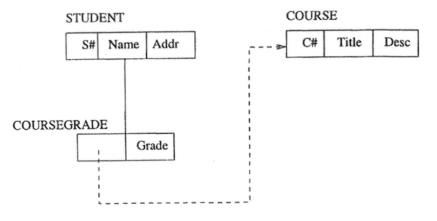

STUDENT

COURSE

COURSEGRADE

Figure 7.2. Using logical parent pointers to remove redundancy

ers (see Figure 7.2). Still, they are not suited for queries such as "Retrieve the students enrolled in the database course cs2102".

The main issue here is the lack of symmetry in hierarchies. This becomes problematic when we need to represent many to many relationships. The IMS database system has built-in functions to provide a symmetric view on the hierarchical structure of data, which reduces unnecessary redundancy and enforces consistency of data.

IMS offers physical pairings. Physical pairing involves introducing a new segment called *COURSEGRADE* that is a physical child of *COURSE* and a logical child of *STUDENT* (see Figure 7.3). The segments *COURSEGRADE* and *STUDENTGRADE* are "paired segments" which are declared to the IMS system.

Note that physical pairing requires the redundant storage of the intersecting data. However, since the segments are paired, when the user inserts an

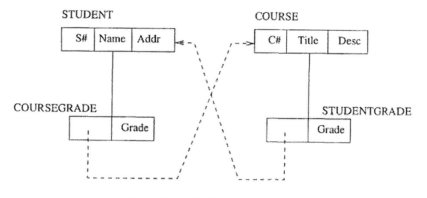

Figure 7.3. Physical pairing in IMS

occurrence of either one, IMS will automatically create the corresponding occurrence of the other.

7.3 Redundancy in ORA-SS Schema Diagram

We now examine the different kinds of data redundancy that can be present in documents based on XML schemas. Some forms of redundancy are desirable while other are not.

1 Data redundancy occurs in an instance if there is a many to many relationship type, and the participating child object class has attributes.

Consider a schema where the courses that a student is enrolled in are nested within student, as shown in Figure 7.4. Every time an instance of course is repeated, the values of the attributes of that course are repeated. Although this kind of redundancy is usually described as undesirable, it is not always necessary to remove this kind of redundancy. The advantage of this redundancy is that it can improve the retrieval performance, and it can be retained if the storage space that the duplicated data takes up is small and if the data that is replicated is not going to be updated often.

2 Data redundancy occurs if data is replicated to handle symmetric queries.

Consider an XML document that describes the courses that students are enrolled in. There are many ways to organize this data. A schema that is suitable for answering queries about courses that a student is enrolled in, and also queries about students enrolled in a course is shown in Figure 7.5. This schema is suitable for symmetric queries. The relationship types *cs* and *sc* represent the same real world relationship, namely the relationship between students and courses, but this information is duplicated in the hierarchical storage structure. Duplicating this information is a disadvantage, but it is duplicated only once.

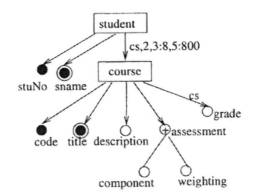

Figure 7.4. Many to many relationship type

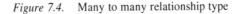
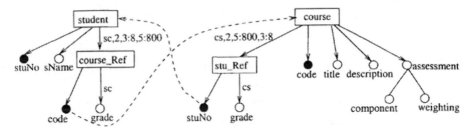

Figure 7.5. Symmetric relationship type

3 Data redundancy occurs in an instance if a relationship type is nested under an many to many relationship type in the semistructured (or hierarchical) schema.

Consider an example with three object classes *project, member* and *publication,* and binary relationship types representing *members* belonging to *projects,* and *publications* belonging to *members.* A *member* can be involved in one or more *projects.* If this is modeled with *member* as a subelement of *project,* and *publication* as a subelement of *member* then the same set of *publications* will be duplicated for each *project* the *member* is involved in. See Figure 7.6. This kind of redundancy is undesirable, but ternary relationships are often represented this way in models that are unable to represent n-ary relationships $(n > 2)$.

4 Data redundancy occurs in an instance if an attribute(s) is replicated.

Duplicating attributes is appropriate if the value of the attribute is unlikely to change, and the duplication of the information improves the performance of a query. Consider the schema in Figure 7.5, where the attribute *grade* is duplicated. Once a grade is awarded to a student in a course, it is unlikely

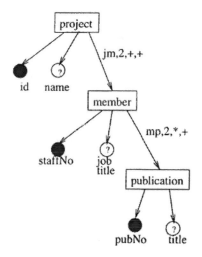

Figure 7.6. Relationship type nested under many to many relationship type

to change. If instead of replicating the attribute *grade*, the information is stored only once for relationship type *sc* but not for relationship type *cs*, the performance of a query that lists the course code and grade for every course for each student does not change, but the performance of a query that lists the students and grades for every course is slower.

5 Data redundancy occurs in an instance if a derived attribute is precomputed and stored or an aggregate function is precomputed and stored.

In Figure 7.7 the value for *grade* is derived from the attribute *mark* while the attribute *average(mark)* is an aggregate capturing the average mark for each student. Storing the precomputed *grade* and *average(mark)* improves the performance of queries that involve these attributes, while possibly degrading the speed of updates.

6 Data redundancy occurs if data is replicated to handle recursive queries.

The relationship types between subordinates and their manager where subordinate and manager are modeled as staff is shown in Figure 7.8(a). This schema is suitable for queries that ask who is the manager of a particular subordinate, but unsuitable for a query that asks for the subordinates of a particular manager. The schema in Figure 7.8(b) with the duplicated reference is suitable for both types of query. To improve performance it is appropriate to include an extra reference.

7 Data redundancy occurs in the data instance if the same object class or object classes occur in different relationship types.

146

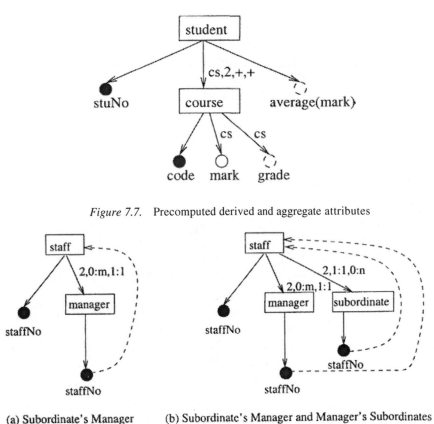

Figure 7.7. Precomputed derived and aggregate attributes

(a) Subordinate's Manager   (b) Subordinate's Manager and Manager's Subordinates

Figure 7.8. Replication of references for recursive query

Consider an XML document that describes people's roles in a University. One part of the document may contain information about projects that staff members work on, while another part may contain information about departments that staff members work in. Parts of the ORA-SS schema diagram are shown in Figure 7.9. The advantage of duplicating the information as shown is the performance of retrieval of the data, while the disadvantage is in maintaining the consistency of the copies.

7.4   Replicated NF in ORA-SS

To define when some replication is desirable in ORA-SS schemas we use concepts analogous to strong functional dependencies and replicated 3NF in relational databases, which are reviewed in Section 7.1. The intuition that we capture is that if an attribute is seldom changed then its replication will not cause any update anomalies.

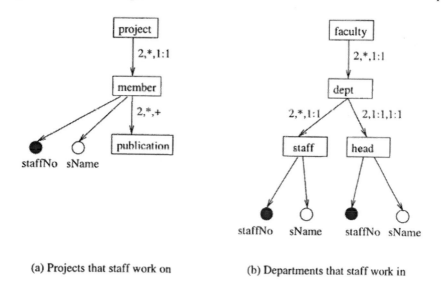

(a) Projects that staff work on   **(b) Departments that staff work in**

Figure 7.9. Duplication of staff information in document

Consider the following example. The schema in Figure 7.10(a) has object classes *course, student* and *tutor*. This schema is not an NF ORA-SS schema, since both *cs* and *cst* are many to many relationship types. The corresponding NF ORA-SS schema diagram is shown in Figure 7.10(b). If the data is stored using the NF ORA-SS schema, then to answer the query listing the names of all the students taking "CS1102" involves following a reference, which is slower than calculating the parent/child relationship. Since the *name* of a student does not change often, there is little overhead in replicating the *name*. The overhead is the extra space taken.

To define this kind of replication more formally we need to define a new kind of normal form, which we call replicated NF ORA-SS schema diagrams.

Definition 7.2 *Let X be an attribute. Attribute X could be single-valued or multivalued, and it could be an attribute of an object class or a relationship type. We say that X is a* **relatively stable attribute** *if the value of X will not be updated, or if the update need not be performed in real-time.*

For example, the attribute *title* of object class *course,* and *name* of object class *student* are not likely to be updated often and any update does not need to happen in real-time. Thus, we say that these attributes are relatively stable attributes.

Definition 7.3 *Let R be a relationship type with participating object classes* $O_1, \ldots, O_n$. *We say that a relationship type R is a* **relatively stable relation-**

148

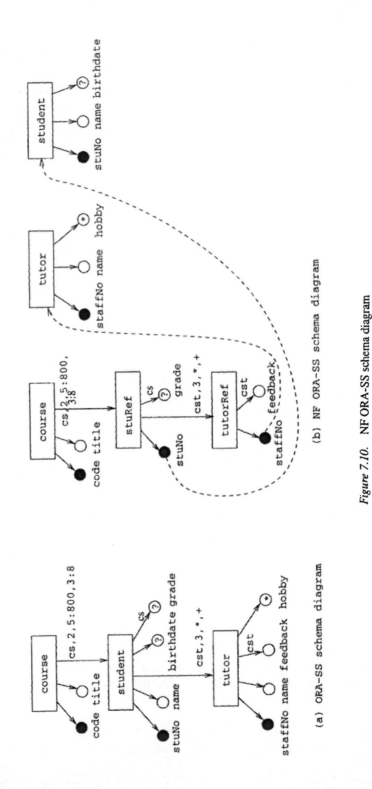

Figure 7.10. NF ORA-SS schema diagram

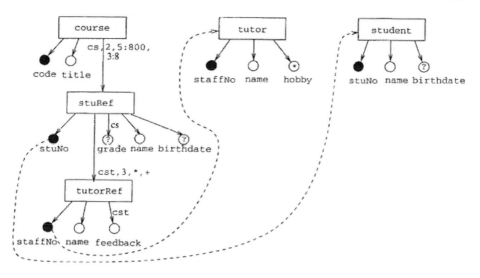

Figure 7.11. Replicated NF ORA-SS schema diagram with allowed replication of relatively stable attributes, *name* and *birthdate*

ship type *if the objects participating in the relationships do not change, or if the changes need not be performed in real-time.*

For example, the relationship type *spouse* and the *part-subpart* relationship types whose participating objects change infrequently are relatively stable relationship types.

Definition 7.4 *Let D be an ORA-SS schema diagram. Let D' be a copy of D where the relatively stable attributes and relatively stable relationship types and their participating object classes have been omitted. We say that an ORA-SS schema diagram D is a* **replicated NF ORA-SS schema,** *if the ORA-SS schema diagram D is an NF ORA-SS schema diagram.*

Consider again the ORA-SS schema diagram in Figure 7.10(b). The attributes *name* and *birthdate* of student, and *name* of tutor are unlikely to change so they are relatively stable attributes. The attribute *hobby* of tutor is likely to change, and is not a relatively stable attribute. In the schema in Figure 7.11 the relatively stable attributes are replicated. If the replicated attributes are removed, that is, *name* and *birthdate* from *stuRef,* and *name* from *tutorRef,* then the resulting schema is the same as the NF ORA-SS schema diagram in Figure 7.10(b). Hence, the ORA-SS schema diagram in Figure 7.11 is a replicated NF ORA-SS schema diagram.

Replicated NF ORA-SS schema diagrams have the advantage that certain class of queries will execute faster. Update, insertion and deletion anomalies

150

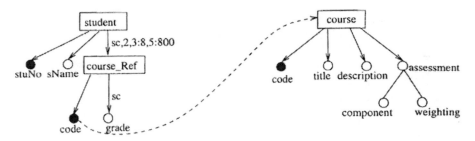

Figure 7.12. NF ORA-SS Schema Diagram

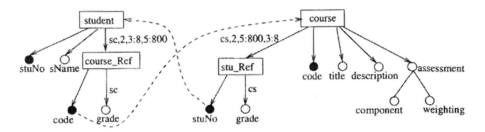

Figure 7.13. Symmetric relationship type

will not occur as long as strict updating policies are adhered to, which validate the updates against the primary instance of the attributes and relationships.

7.5 Controlled Pairing in ORA-SS Schema Diagrams

The replication of references can be used to improve the speed of a query. In this section we describe different ways of modeling this replication in a controlled way.

Although the schema in Figure 7.12 is an NF ORA-SS schema diagram, it is not suited to queries such as "List the students enrolled in the database course CS1102 with their grade". In order to answer such queries we replicate the reference between student and course, and the attribute *grade,* as shown in Figure 7.13.

One problem with replicating the grade is that controls must be put in place to ensure whenever a grade is inserted, deleted or updated in one place, the same operation is applied to the copy.

The schema shown in Figure 7.12 is similar to the logical parent pointer example in Section 7.2, while the schema in Figure 7.13 is similar to the physical pairing example in Section 7.2. In IMS, these pairings are declared and maintained automatically by the database system but in other database systems appropriate controls must be put in place to ensure that strict updating policies are adhered to.

An example of pairing, which can be controlled that does not fit the pairing model of IMS, has a binary relationship type that is replicated in a ternary relationship type in order to improve the speed of queries. Consider the binary and ternary relationship represented in Figures 7.14(a) together with (b). The *code* is a number that a supplier uses for a part, which is specific to a supplier. For example, for a part with description *"18 inch bicycle frame"*, one supplier might use the code *"bf18"* while another supplier uses the code *"bicycle –* 2096". The schema shown in Figures 7.14(a) together with (b) is suitable for queries such as:

- List the *sName* of the suppliers who supply parts with description *"18 inch bicycle frame "* to project $p1$.

- List the *code* used by each supplier of the part with description *"18 inch bicycle frame "*.

The first query can be answered by accessing the *sName, part description* and *pNo* in Figure 7.14(b). The second query can be answered by accessing the *code* and *part description* in Figure 7.14(a).
However, this schema is unsuitable for the query:

- List the *code* used by each supplier of the part with description *"18 inch bicycle frame "* supplied to project $p1$.

In order to answer this query, it is necessary to find who the suppliers are of the part with description *"18 inch bicycle frame "* to project $p1$ from Figure 7.14(b) then access the *code* information in Figure 7.14(a).

An alternative organization is shown in Figures 7.14(a) together with (c). This organization improves the performance of the query given above since the attributes can all be accessed in Figure 7.14(c). The duplication of the attribute *code* is possible since the value of the attribute is unlikely to change. Previously we have shown how duplication can be avoided through the use of references. The schema in Figures 7.14(a) together with (c) is an example where references cannot be used. It is possible to include a reference between *part2* and *part* but it is not possible to include a reference between *supplier2* and *supplier* since there will be many supplier objects with the same *sNo*. Strict updating policies must be put in place and adhered to in order to maintain the consistency of the replicated data. For example, if the XML document that conforms to the schema in Figure 7.14(a) together with (c) is stored in an object relational database, then consistency of the replicated data can be achieved by enforcing the following inclusion dependencies. We describe a mapping from an ORA-SS schema diagram to an object relational database in Section 7.8.

152

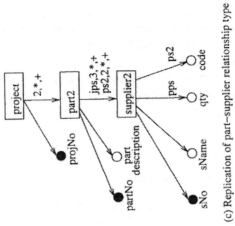

(a) Relationship type between part and supplier

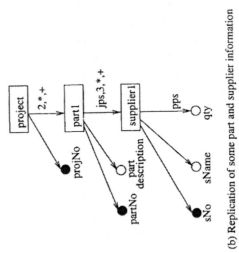

(b) Replication of some part and supplier information

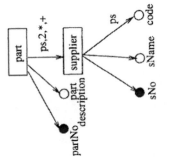

(c) Replication of part–supplier relationship type

Figure 7.14. Repeating relationship type

part2[partNo, part description] ⊆ part[partNo, part description]
supplier2[sNo, sName] ⊆ supplier[sNo, sName]
ps2[partNo, sNo, code] ⊆ ps[partNo, sNo, code]
ps2[partNo, sNo] ⊆ jps[partNo, sNo]

7.6 Measure of Data Replication

As with relational databases, a normalized XML schema design may not provide optimal efficiency. The example below demonstrates how the ORA-SS data model can be used to estimate the cost of replicating data.

Consider the ORA-SS schema diagram in Figure 7.15 that shows the object classes *student* and *course*. A *student* can take 3 to 8 *courses* and a *course* can have 5 to 800 *students*. A *course* has a *code, title, description,* and *assessment*. The *assessment* is a multivalued composite attribute that comprises of *component* and its *weighting*. For example, the *practical component* can have a weighting of 20%, the *test component* can have a weighting of 10%, and the *exam component* can have a weighting of 70%.

Let us assume that

- number of students = 20000

- number of courses = 500

- length of code = 10 bytes

- length of title = 50 bytes

- length of description = 1000 bytes

- length of component = 20 bytes

- length of weighting = 4 bytes

- length of grade = 2 bytes

- length of reference = 10 bytes

The length of each *assessment* is given by the length of *component* and *weighting* = 20 + 4 bytes = 24 bytes. Since we have 3 types of assessment, namely, practical, test, and exam, this attribute occupies a total of 72 bytes. With these information, we can estimate the storage and update cost of modeling data in a particular way.

Let us consider the storage requirements for the course elements. In the schema in Figure 7.15(a), each course is repeated for each student taking the course, which means that the details of each course is stored a minimum of 5 times and a maximum of 800 times (based on the participation constraint

5 : 800). Since the size of each course is at least 10+50+1000+72+2=1134 bytes, the minimum storage requirement is approximately 5*500*1134=2.835 MB, and the maximum storage needed is approximately 800*500*1134=453.6 MB.

On the other hand, if we use a reference pointer to *course* as shown in Figure 7.15(b), then the size of course_Ref is 10+2=12 bytes and the size of course (without the grade) is 1132 bytes, and each course is represented only once, so the maximum storage needs for course is 1*500*1132=0.566 MB and the minimum storage requirement for course_Ref is 5*500*12=0.03 MB and the maximum storage requirement for course_Ref is 800*500*12 = 4.8 MB. The minimum storage requirement of the course information in the schema in Figure 7.15(b) is about 20% of the minimum storage requirement of the course information in Figure 7.15(a), while the maximum storage requirement of the course information in the schema in Figure 7.15(b) is about 1% of the maximum storage requirement of the course information in Figure 7.15(a).

Next, let us consider the update cost. Suppose a *lecturer* updates the *assessment* requirements in a course. Based on the schema in Figure 7.15(a), this would involve updating between 5 and 800 *course* instances. However, only one instance of *course* need to be updated for the schema in Figure 7.15(b). The problem is not only the cost of updating but also ensuring that the *assessment* requirements are updated everywhere they need to be.

Finally, let us examine the cost of performing a query. Traditionally, it is believed that the cost of following a reference is more expensive because of the way data is organized on disk (i.e., one more disk access).

Assume for the moment that we have no indexes, and that a report is frequently printed with *stuNo, sname, code, title, grade*. The schema in Figure 7.15(a) is suitable for answering this query, while the schema in Figure 7.15(b) would require extra disk accesses. However storing the *title* under *course_Ref* improves performance while not taking a large hit on storage, and assuming that a course title does not change, no hit on updating. However, if the query included the description, it is unlikely that the replication of the description is worthwhile since each description is 1000 bytes.

7.7 Guidelines for Physical Semistructured Database Design

We have discussed the different kinds of replication that can occur in semistructured databases, the kinds of replication that can be controlled, how the replication can be managed, and the cost of allowing such replication. In this section we present how this information can be used in the design of database systems for semistructured data.

The steps are similar to the steps followed in relational database design, where requirements are gathered, the schema is normalized, and after the ex-

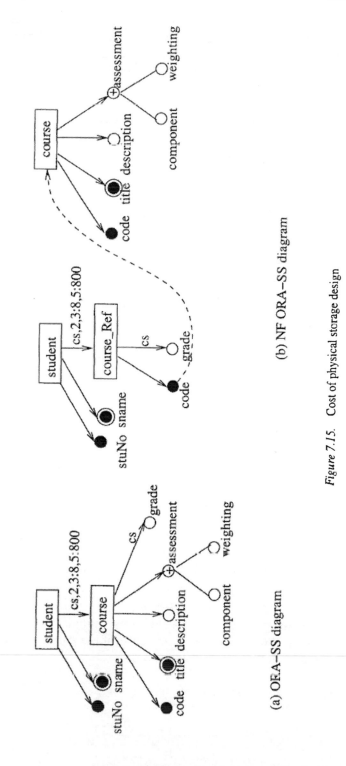

Figure 7.15. Cost of physical storage design

(a) ORA–SS diagram

(b) NF ORA–SS diagram

pected query set is taken into account, some denormalization takes place. We first describe the design process for semistructured databases, then illustrate the process with an example.

The guideline for the design of a semistructured database follows.

Step 1. An ORA-SS schema is derived either from real world requirements, or extracted from XML documents via an ORA-SS instance diagram.

Step 2. The ORA-SS schema diagram is normalized to a NF ORA-SS schema diagram.

Step 3. A set of suggested replications is derived from the expected query set.

Step 4. For each suggested replication that involves relatively stable attributes or relatively stable relationship types, consider the storage cost required for the replication. It is not necessary to consider update cost since relatively stable attributes and relationship types do not change often.

Step 5. For the other suggested replications, consider both the storage and update cost of the replication.

Step 6. For all replications ensure that the necessary controls are put in place to maintain the integrity of the data. For example, for relatively stable attributes and relationship types, it is necessary to enforce that replicated data is consistent when the data is inserted. For the pairing required for symmetric queries, a reference is duplicated. The consistency of this duplication must be enforced when information is inserted, deleted or updated. In this case, the performance of the consistency checking is predictable since the references are duplicated only once.

The following example illustrates the guidelines described above.

Step 1. The ORA-SS schema diagram in Figure 7.15(a) captures the real world constraints that are to be modeled. Designing a database based on this schema leads to redundancies in the instance of the database, which in turn leads to insertion, deletion and update anomalies.

Step 2. Using the algorithm in Chapter 5, the schema is normalized. The resulting NF ORA-SS schema diagram is shown in Figure 7.15(b).

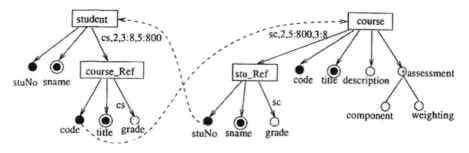

Figure 7.16. Resulting ORA-SS Schema with controlled replication

Step 3. The following queries are frequently asked:

Query 1: list the name and grade of students taking the course with code *CS*1102, along with the title of the course

Query 2: list the title of the courses taken by student with stuNo *stu*125 along with the grade the student has scored in each course.

The schema in Figure 7.15(b) is suitable for a query that asks for the grades of courses taken by student with stuNo *stu*125, but if the query also asks for the title of the course (as in Query 2), a reference is followed slowing the performance. The performance of Query 2 will improve if title is replicated under course_Ref. The schema in Figure 7.15(b) is not suitable for Query 1 since each student object must be read, and the code of the courses the student is enrolled in must be inspected. The performance of this query is improved if a reference is added between course and student, pairing the reference from student to course. In order to improve the performance of this query further, the title of the course can be stored as an attribute of *course_Ref*. The suggested replication is shown in Figure 7.16. The *name* of the *student* and the *title* of the *course* are relatively stable attributes.

Step 4. We now calculate the extra maximum storage cost between Figure 7.15(b) and Figure 7.16, based on the following information:

- number of students = 20000

- number of courses = 500

- length of title = 50 bytes

- length of sname = 30 bytes

- length of grade = 2 bytes

- length of reference = 10 bytes

The maximum storage required for the replication of

- *sname* is $8 * 20000 * 30 \approx 8$ MB

- *title* is $800 * 500 * 50 \approx 20$ MB

- *grade* for the relationship type *sc* is $8 * 20000 * 2 \approx 0.320$ MB.

- the reference from *stu_Ref* to *student* is $8 * 20000 * 10 \approx 1.6$ MB.

The maximum amount of extra storage required is $8 + 20 + .32 + 1.6 \approx 30$ MB which is ten times more than the maximum storage requirement for the schema in Figure 7.15(b).

Step 5. We now calculate the update cost of the new schema. We do not consider the update cost of relatively stable attributes, such as *title* of *course* and *sname* of *student,* since by definition they are unlikely to be updated. So the only extra update cost incurred is the cost of maintaining the student grade. Whenever the value of a grade of relationship type *cs* is updated, the value of a grade attribute of relationship type *sc* will also need to be updated. Because the grade is replicated only once, the update cost is doubled. Similarly, when students withdraw and add courses, because the reference is replicated only once, the update cost is doubled.

The costs of performing the queries in the expected query set have decreased. The addition of the attribute *title* to object class *course_Ref* improves the performance of Query 2. The addition of object class *stu_Ref* with attribute *sname* and the relationship type attribute *grade* improves the performance of Query 1. The addition of the extra reference improves any ad hoc queries that ask about *students* within *courses*.

Step 6. It is important that dependencies between the data are defined and the necessary controls are put in place to maintain the consistency of the replicated data automatically. For example, whenever a *grade* of the relationship type *cs* is updated, the corresponding *grade* of relationship type *sc* must also be updated. Similarly when a student enrolls in a course, a reference must be included to indicate the courses the student has enrolled in, the replicated reference must be introduced, and the student's *sname* must be updated in *stu_Ref*.

7.8 Storage of Documents in an Object Relational Database

In order to design an efficient organization of data in a data store, it is essential to have an algorithm that maps the logical data model to the data store. In

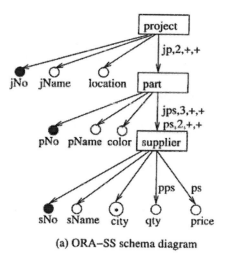

Object relations
project(jNo, jName, location)
part(pNo, pName, color)
supplier(sNo, sName, (city)*)

Relationship relations
ps(sNo, pNo, price)
jps(sNo, pNo, jNo, qty)

Constraints
jps[sNo, pNo] ⊆ ps[sNo, pNo]

(a) ORA–SS schema diagram   (b) Object Relational Schema

Figure 7.17. Mapping ORA-SS Schema Diagram to object relational model

this section, we outline an algorithm that maps ORA-SS schema diagrams to the object relational model. The algorithm demonstrates how semistructured data can efficiently and consistently be stored in an object relational database management system like Oracle 8*i*.

Figure 7.17 shows an ORA-SS schema diagram and the associated object relational schema. The latter can be obtained by the following mapping algorithm:

1 for each object class, create a (possibly nested) relation where the identifier of the object class is the key of the relation. Each single-valued attribute of the object class becomes a single-valued attribute of the relation, while each multivalued attribute becomes a set-valued attribute (i.e. nested relation) in the relation. Each reference is a foreign key in the relation.

2 for each relationship type, create a (possibly nested) relation where all the identifiers of the participating object classes of the relationship type are single-valued attributes of the relation. If the identifiers of $O_1, \ldots, O_n$ form the key of the relationship type then the identifiers of $O_1, \ldots, O_n$ form the key of the relation created. Each single-valued attribute of the relationship type is a single-valued attribute of the relation, and each multivalued attribute is a set-valued attribute (i.e. nested relation) in the relation.

Note that the ORA-SS schema diagram enables the mapping algorithm to correctly associate the attribute *price* with part and supplier in the *ps* relation, and the attribute *quantity* with project, part and supplier in the *jps* relation.

7.9 Summary

While the process of transforming an ORA-SS schema diagram to an NF ORA-SS schema diagram can lead to databases that have no replicated data which in turn leads to a reduction in anomalies, the addition of references may adversely degrade the performance of queries on the database.

In this chapter, we have addressed how replication can be added back into a schema in a controlled manner in order to improve the performance of queries that are frequently asked. We have reviewed how attributes that seldom change are dealt with in relational databases, and how pairings are maintained automatically in hierarchical IMS databases for answering symmetric queries efficiently.

We have described the kinds of replication that can arise in semistructured databases, and how the replication of relatively stable attributes and relationship types can be added, and how pairings between object classes can be maintained. These concepts have roots in the approaches taken by relational and IMS databases to deal with replication and answering symmetric queries respectively. The costs incurred in the replication of data in semistructured databases include the storage cost, the update cost and the performance cost. Recognizing that some attributes and relationship types are relatively stable gives a more realistic picture of the update cost.

Guidelines for semistructured database design are introduced and demonstrated, from requirements gathering, through conceptual modeling to physical modeling. Finally, we have outlined an algorithm for storing XML documents efficiently and consistently in a traditional database system.

Chapter 8

CONCLUSION

Web applications typically deal with data that is semistructured. With the increased number of web applications, and the increasing amount of data that is produced and consumed by these applications, there is a need for processes that are guaranteed to maintain the consistency of the data. One such process is the design of a data repository that manages semistructured data.

The steps in the design of a repository for semistructured data are as follows:

1. Choose a data model that is able to represent the semantics necessary for modeling semistructured data,

2. Capture the semantics of the data that will be stored, either by:

   (a) extracting the schema from a set of documents and discovering the semantics in a data model, or

   (b) studying the constraints in the real world and capturing them in a data model,

3. Reorganize the schema into an NF ORA-SS schema diagram to avoid replication of data in the XML documents,

4. Consider the typical query set and reorganize the schema to improve the performance of typical queries, perhaps by introducing controlled replication of data,

5. Consider the users of the system and define views over the data for individual users or groups of users.

These steps are outlined in Figure 8.1, and the chapters in the book that correspond to the steps are highlighted with each step.

162

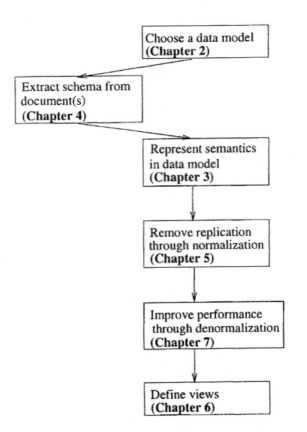

Figure 8.1. Steps in the Design of Repositories for Semistructured Data

Because of the rich semantics that can be represented in the ORA-SS data model, it can be used as the foundation for other work in the semistructured data field. We list some further possibilities here:

- We have discussed how the ORA-SS data model can be used to recognize if there is redundancy in a semistructured data repository. Hence, further normal forms for semistructured data and the underlying theory could be defined based on the ORA-SS data model. The ORA-SS instance diagram can also be used to capture how the instance of the data needs to change after the schema has been restructured.

- We have shown how semistructured data and XML data can be mapped to the object relational data model. More work needs to be done to design efficient storage organizations for other data models (such as the object oriented and relational data models) with indexes based on the ORA-SS schema.

- The ORA-SS data model can be used to identify which views are meaningful. This work can be extended to define how materialized views are updated, what updates to views are valid, and how updates to views are propagated to the underlying data.

- Query optimization involves rewriting queries into a form that will execute faster than the original query. Semantic query optimization involves rewriting the query based on the semantics of the data to improve query performance. The ORA-SS schema diagram can provide the necessary semantics, and could be used for semantic query optimization in semistructured data repositories.

- The ORA-SS data model provides a user-friendly way to visualize the instance and schema of a semistructured data store, and can be used in tools that require data visualization. Preliminary work in this area is presented in [Ni and Ling, 2003].

- The ORA-SS data model provides a simple and standard way for representing semantics which can be used for data integration. A large part of data integration involves finding equivalences or matches between two or more schema. The problem of finding equivalences of object classes, relationship types and attributes between diagrams is very complex. It is easier to find equivalences automatically or semi-automatically with a good understanding of the underlying semantics of the data.

This page intentionally left blank

Appendix A
ORA-SS Notation

The following tables summarize the notation of ORA-SS diagrams.

notation	description
a	object class with name a
$\overset{(x)}{b}$	attribute b, where x represents the cardinality, ? is 0 or 1, + is 1 or more, * is 0 or more, and the default value for x is 1.
$\overset{(x)}{b}$ (with box and ordering arrow)	attribute b where the ordering of the value of the attributes is important. x is either + or *, and the default value is *.
composite tree (a, b, c)	composite attribute a with component attributes b and c
disjunctive tree (a, b, c)	disjunctive attribute a is either b or c
● c	identifier/primary key c
◉ d	candidate key d

notation	description
	composite identifier/primary key
	composite candidate key
	derived attribute
	attribute with unknown structure or whose structure is heterogeneous
	the ordering on the attributes of object class a is important
R (object class list), $n,a{:}b,c{:}d,<$	relationship type with name R, with participating objects *object class list,* of degree n, where the participation of the parent has minimum a and maximum b, and the child has minimum c and maximum d, and the ordering of the object classes is important. The name is optional. The object class list is optional and is included only if the object classes of the relationship type are separated by object class(es) not relevant to the relationship type. The default degree is 2, default parent participation constraint is $0 : m$, default child participation constraint is $1 : n$, and default on ordering is no ordering.
$R, n,a{:}b,c{:}d$	attribute x belongs to relationship type R. The default (without label R on the edge) shows that attribute x belongs to object class e.

notation	description
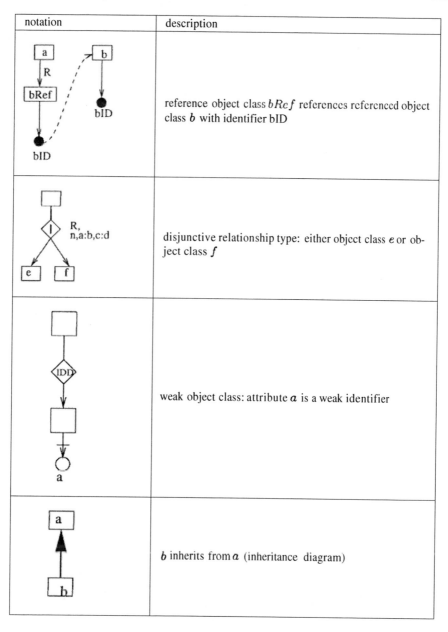	reference object class $bRef$ references referenced object class b with identifier bID
	disjunctive relationship type: either object class e or object class f
	weak object class: attribute a is a weak identifier
	b inherits from a (inheritance diagram)

This page intentionally left blank

References

Abiteboul, S. (1999). On views and XML. In *Proceedings of 18th ACM Symposium on Principles of Database Systems.*

Abiteboul, S., Amann, B., Cluet, S., Eyal, A., Mignet, L., and Milo, T. (1999a). Active views for electronic commerce. In *Proceedings of 25th International Conference on Very Large Data Bases.*

Abiteboul, S., Buneman, P., and Suciu, D. (1999b). *Data On the Web-From Relational to Semistructured Data and XML.* Morgan Kaufman Publishers, San Francisco, California.

Apparao, V. and Byrne, S. (1 October 1998). Document object model (DOM) level 1 specification. W3C Recommendation.

Arenas, M. and Libkin, L. (2004). A normal form for XML documents. *ACM Trans. Database Syst.,* 29(1):195–232.

Baru, C. K., Gupta, A., Ludascher, B., Marciano, R., Papakonstantinou, Y., Velikhov, P., and Chu, V. (1999). XML-based information mediation with MIX. In *SIGMOD 1999, Proceedings ACM SIGMOD International Conference on Management of Data.*

Bray, T., Paoli, J., and Sperberg-McQueen, C. M. (Oct. 2000). Extensible markup language (XML) 1.0. 2nd edition. http://www.w3.org/TR/REC-xml.

Buneman, P., Davidson, S., Fan, W., Hara, C., and Tan, W.C. (2001a). Keys for XML. In *Proceedings of the Tenth International World Wide Web Conference.*

Buneman, P., Davidson, S., Fan, W., Hara, C., and Tan, W.C. (2001b). Reasoning about keys for XML. In *International Workshop on Database Programming Languages.*

Carey, M. J., Kiernan, J., Shanmugasundaram, J., Shekita, E. J., and Subramanian, S. N. (2000). Xperanto: Middleware for publishing object-relational data as XML documents. In *Proceedings of 26th International Conference on Very Large Data Bases,* pages 646–648.

Chen, Y.B., Ling, T.W., and Lee, M.L. (2002). Designing valid XML views. In *Proceedings of 21st International Conference on Conceptual Modeling.*

Christophides, V., Cluet, S., and Simeon, J. (2000). On wrapping query languages and efficient XML integration. In *Proceedings of the 2000 ACM SIGMOD International Conference on Management of Data,* pages 141–152.

Cluet, S., Veltri, P., and Vodislav, D. (2001). Views in a large scale XML repository. In *Proceedings of 27th International Conference on Very Large Data Bases,* pages 271–280.

Date, C. J. (1975). *An Introduction to Database Systems.* Addison Wesley, 1st edition.

Deutsch, A., Fernandez, M., and Suciu, D. (1999). Storing semistructured data with STORED. In *ACM SIGMOD,* pages 431–442.

170

Deutsch, A. and Tannen, V. (2003). Mars: A system for publishing xml from mixed and redundant storag e. In *VLDB*.

Dobbie, G., Wu, X., Ling, T.W., and Lee, M.L. (2000). ORA-SS: An object-relationship-attribute model for semi-structured data. Technical Report TR21/00, School of Computing, National University of Singapore.

Embley, D.W. and Mok, W.Y. (2001). Developing XML documents with guaranteed "good" properties. In *Proc. of 20th International Conference on Conceptual Modeling*.

Fan, W. and Simeon, J. (2000). Integrity Constraints for XML. In *Proceedings of the Nineteenth ACM SIGMOD-SIGACT-SIGART Symposium on Principles of Database Systems, Dallas, Texas, USA*, pages 23–34. ACM.

Fernandez, M., Tan, W., and Suciu, D. (2000). SilkRoute: Trading between relations and XML. In *Proceedings of the 9th International World Wide Web Conference*.

Florescu, D. and Kossmann, D. (1999). Storing and querying XML data using an RDBMS. *IEEE Data Engineering Bulletin*, 22(3):27–34.

Goldman, R. and Widom, J. (1997). Dataguides: Enabling query formulation and optimization in semistructured databases. In *Proc. of 23rd International Conference on Very Large Data Bases*, pages 436–445.

ISO/IEC (2000). Information technology - text and office systems - regular language description for XML (RELAX) - part 1: RELAX core. DTR 22250-1.

Lee, D. and Chu, W. (2000). Constraints-preserving transformation from XML document type definition to relational schema. In *Proc. 19th International Conference on Conceptual Modeling*, pages 323–338.

Lee, S.Y., Lee, M.L., Ling, T.W., and Kalinichenko, L.A. (1999). Designing good semi-structured databases. In *Proc. 18th International Conference on Conceptual Modeling*, pages 131–145.

Ling, T. W. (1989). A normal form for sets of not-necessarily normalized relations. In *Proceedings of the 22nd Hawaii International Conference on System Sciences*, pages 578–586. IEEE Computer Society Press.

Ling, T. W. and Yan, L. L. (1994). NF-NR: A practical normal form for nested relations. *Journal of Systems Integration*, 4:309–340.

Ling, T.W. (1985). A normal form for entity-relationship diagrams. In *Proc. 4th International Conference on Entity-Relationship Approach*.

Ling, T.W., Goh, C.H., and Lee, M.L. (1996). Extending classical functional dependencies for physical database design. *Information and Software Technology*, 38:601–608.

Ling, T.W. and Teo, P.K. (1993). Inheritance conflicts in object-oriented systems. In *Proc. 4th International Conference on Database and Expert Systems Applications, DEXA '93*, pages 189–200.

Mani, M., Lee, D., and Muntz, R.R. (2001). Semantic data modeling using XML schemas. In *Proc. of 20th International Conference on Conceptual Modeling*, pages 149–163.

Manolescu, I., Florescu, D., and Kossmann, D. (2001). Answering XML queries on heterogeneous data sources. In *Proceedings of 27th International Conference on Very Large Data Bases*, pages 241–250.

McHugh, J., Abiteboul, S., Goldman, R., Quass, D., and Widom, J. (1997). Lore: A database management system for semistructured data. *SIGMOD Record*, 26(3):54–66.

Mo, Y. and Ling, T.W. (2002). Storing and maintaining semistructured data efficiently in an object-relational database. In *Proc. of 3rd International Conference on Web Information Systems Engineering (WISE 2002)*, pages 247–256.

Ni, W. and Ling, T.W. (2003). GLASS: A graphical query language for semi-structured data. In *Proc. of Eighth International Conference on Database Systems for Advanced Applications (DASFAA '03)*.

Ozsoyoglu, Z.M. and Yuan, L.Y. (1987). A new normal form for nested relations. *ACM Transaction on Database Systems,* 12(1).

Shanmugasundaram, J., Tufte, K., Zhang, C., He, G., DeWitt, D.J., and Naughton, J.F. (1999). Relational databases for querying XML documents: Limitations and opportunities. In *Proc. of 25th International Conference on Very Large Data Bases,* pages 79–90.

Suciu, D. (1998). Semistructured data and XML. In *Proc, of 5th International Conference on Foundations of Data Organization.*

Thompson, H.S., Beech, D., Maloney, M., and (Eds), N. Mendelson (May 2001). XML Schema Part 1: Structures. http://www.w3.org/TR/xmlschcina-1.

Wang, Q.Y., Xu, J.X., and Wong, K.F. (2000). Approximate graph schema extraction for semistructured data. In *Proc. of 7th International Conference on Extending Database Technology.*

Widom, J. (1999). Data management for XML: Research directions. *IEEE Data Engineering Bulletin,* 22(3):44–52.

Wu, X., Ling, T.W., Lee, M.L., and Dobbic, G. (2001a). Designing semistructured databases using ORA-SS model. In *Proc. of 2nd International Conference on Web Information Systems Engineering.*

Wu, X.Y., Ling, T.W., Lee, S.Y., Lee, M.L., and Dobbie, G. (November 2001b). NF-SS: A normal form for semistructured schemata. In *Proceedings of the International Workshop on Data Semantics in Web Information Systems (DASWIS/ER2001).* Springer-Verlag.

This page intentionally left blank

Index

About the Authors

Dr Gillian DOBBIE is currently an Associate Professor in the Department of Computer Science at the University of Auckland, New Zealand, and Deputy Director of the Software Engineering Programme.
[See http://www.cs.auckland.ac.nz/people/profile.php?id=gdob002]

She received a Ph.D. from the University of Melbourne, an M.Tech.(Hons) and B.Tech.(Hons) in Computer Science from Massey University. She has lectured at Massey University, the University of Melbourne, and Victoria University of Wellington, and held visiting research positions at Griffith University and the National University of Singapore.

Her research interests include formal foundations for databases, object oriented databases, semistructured databases, logic and databases, data warehousing, data mining, access control, e-commerce and data modeling. She has published 27 international refereed journal and conference papers. Some of the publications are listed in http://www.informatik.uni- trier.de/ ley/db/indices/a-tree/d/Dobbie:Gillian.html.

She is programme co-chair on ADC05 and ADC06, and has served as programme co-chair on WEBH2001 and WEBH2002. She has served on programme committees for many international conferences including DOOD97, ADC98, DaWaK01, WISE2002, and ACE2003, and has refereed papers for international journals such as TPLP and VLDB.

Dr. Mong Li LEE is currently an Assistant Professor in the School of Computing at the National University of Singapore. She received her Ph.D. degree in Computer Science from the National University of Singapore in 1999. Her thesis examines translation, integration and update issues in a federated database environment. She was awarded the IEEE Singapore Information Technology Gold Medal for being the top student in the Computer Science program in 1989.

Mong Li joined the Department of Computer Science, National University of Singapore, as a Senior Tutor from 1989 to 1999. In 1999, she was appointed Fellow in the School of Computing and lectured Introduction to Programming in JAVA, a Lecture-on-Demand module. She was a Visiting Fellow at the Computer Science Department, University of Wisconsin-Madison and Consultant at QUIQ Incorporated, USA, from September 1999 to August 2000.

Her research interests include the cleaning and integration of heterogeneous and semistructured data, performance database issues in dynamic environments, and medical informatics. Her work has been published in ACM SIGMOD, ACM SIGKDD, VLDB, ICDE and ER conferences. She is a co-Editor for the Proceedings of the 17th International Conference on Conceptual Modeling (ER 1998) and Proceedings of VLDB 2002 Workshop EEXTT and CAiSE 2002 Workshop DIWeb (LNCS #2590, Springer-Verlag). She is a Program Committee member of VLDB (2002, 2003, 2004), DASFAA (2003, 2004) and ER (1998, 1999, 2001, 2003, 2004) and a reviewer for IEEE TKDE and DAMI journals.

Dr. Tok Wang LING is a Professor of the Department of Computer Science, School of Computing at the National University of Singapore, Singapore. He was the Head of Information Technology Division, Deputy Head of the Department of Information Systems and Computer Science, and a Vice Dean of the School. Before joining the University as a lecturer in 1979, he was a scientific staff at Bell Northern Research, Ottawa, Canada. He received his Ph.D. and M.Math., both in Computer Science, from Waterloo University, Canada, and B.Sc.(1 Hons) in Mathematics from Nanyang University, Singapore.

His research interests include Data Modeling, Entity-Relationship Approach, Object-Oriented Data Model, Normalization Theory, Logic and Database, Integrity Constraint Checking, Semistructured Data Model, and Data Warehousing. He has published more than 150 international journal/conference papers and chapters in books, mainly in data modeling. He also co-edited 12 conference and workshop proceedings.

He organized and served as program committee co-chair of DASFAA'95, DOOD'95, ER'98, WISE 2002, and ER 2003. He organized and served/serves as conference co-chair of Human.Society @Internet conference in 2001 and 2003, WAIM 2004, ER 2004, and DASFAA 2005. He served/serves as workshop co-chair of DOOD'95 Post-Conference Workshops, the 8th International Parallel Computing Workshop, and the International Workshop on Conceptual Model-directed Web Information Integration and Mining held in conjunction with ER 2004.

He serves/served on the program committees of more than 100 international database conferences since 1985. He is currently the chair of the steering committee of International Conference on Database Systems for Advanced Applications (DASFAA), a member of the steering committee of International Conference on Conceptual Modeling (ER) and the International Conference on Human.Society@Internet. He was chair and vice chair of the steering committee of ER conference and a member of the steering committee of International Conference on Deductive and Object-Oriented Databases (DOOD).

He is an editor of the journal Data & Knowledge Engineering, International Journal of Cooperative Information Systems, Journal of Database Management, Journal of Data Semantics, and World Wide Web: Internet and Web Information Systems. He is also an advisor of the ACM Transactions on Internet Technology. He is a member of ACM, IEEE, and Singapore Computer Society.

CPSIA information can be obtained at www.ICGtesting.com
Printed in the USA
LVOW070335150312

273186LV00004B/81/P